MANAGING
the people side of
INNOVATION

MANAGING
the people side of
INNOVATION

8 RULES FOR ENGAGING
MINDS AND HEARTS

A. J. CHOPRA

KUMARIAN
PRESS

Managing the People Side of Innovation: 8 Rules for Engaging Minds and Hearts

Published 1999 in the United States of America by Kumarian Press, Inc.,
14 Oakwood Avenue, West Hartford, Connecticut 06119-2127 USA.

Production and design by The Sarov Press, Stratford, Connecticut.
The text of this book is set in Palatino 11/14.5.

Printed in the United States of America on
acid-free paper by Thomson-Shore, Inc.
Text printed with soy-based ink.

The paper used in this publication meets the minimum requirements
of the American National Standard for Information Sciences—Permanence of
∞ Paper for Printed Library Materials, ANSI Z39.48–1984.

Library of Congress Cataloging-in-Publication Data
Chopra, A. J.
    Managing the people side of innovation : 8 rules for engaging
minds and hearts / A.J. Chopra.
        p.   cm.
    ISBN 1–56549–098–3 (alk. paper)
    1. Organizational change.   2. Organizational learning.
3. Technological innovations—Management.   I. Title.
HD58.8.C477   1999
658.4'06—dc21   99–22634

03   02   01   00   99   5   4   3   2   1   First Printing 1999

TO
MY MOTHER

AUTHOR'S NOTE

The stories in this book are all based on things I've seen in my work. But names and in many cases the settings and other details are made up to protect the identities of the individuals and organizations involved.

Contents

ACKNOWLEDGMENTS

Thanks to Bill Gordon, George Prince, and Cavas Gobhai for introducing me to and helping me to get started in the line of work that led to this book.

For helpful comments and suggestions at various stages of the book's development, many thanks to:

Robert Christian, Nina Ryan, Elizabeth Eisler, Roger Golde, Kyra Montagu, Kathy Herald, Krishna Sondhi, Linda Field, Brian Ward, Peter McKinney, Katy Fleury, Houda Samaha, MaryEllen Broganer, and Carol Christian.

It took me a lot longer than I thought it would to write this book. For encouraging me to keep going, a very special thanks to my wife, Elizabeth Eisler, and to Hank Grant, Kate Lamonica, Charlotte Lim, Robert Lee, Charlene Pasco, Graham Pratt, and Shirley Quek.

1

■ Introduction

innovate: to introduce something new;
make changes in anything established.

Managing Innovation: Why You Need to Be Good at It

Look at any organization's mission or vision statement, or at any big message from its president to its people. Odds are you won't see one that doesn't mention innovation (or the thing that drives it: change). Not surprising, given the pressure on all organizations — public and private, business and non-profit — to deliver "new and improved" products and services, and to deliver them faster and cheaper than the competition.

This pressure on your organization makes innovation a part of your job in two ways, one more obvious than the other.

It's easy to see that it's become part of your job when you have to spend time managing or being part of an effort to design and deliver a new product, or to cut costs, or to "reengineer" the way something is done.

What's not so obvious is that the kind of performance expected from the organization is also expected from *you*. You and your unit or team are expected to deliver better "goods and services" tomorrow than you did yesterday, and to do it more cost effectively. You are expected to do these things not just once but continuously, in an ongoing way. The expectation may not be stated explicitly, but it's there nevertheless. Your job is a business in microcosm, and you have to run it innovatively.

The Focus of This Book: What It's Not, What It Is

Managing innovation means getting people (including yourself) to look for better ways of doing things. And getting them to do a good job of implementing these "better" ideas, whether their own or those of others.

You can manage innovation by doing things at one or both of two levels, the *organizational* and the *operational*.

The organizational level (what this book is *not* about)

Here you are concerned with the way people think about and do things *in general*. The things you do at this level are aimed either at creating a culture that is innovation friendly, or at redirecting people's creative energies when the goals or the circumstances of the organization change.

When competition was introduced in the U.S. telephone industry the people at AT&T had to change their way of thinking from one that was O.K. for a technology driven company, to the very different one needed for one that was market driven. Senior managers in some of the companies I've worked with had to figure out how to change the culture from one that placed a premium on maintaining business methods and not rocking the boat, to one that encouraged people to try new things and make a few waves.

Managing innovation at this level means tinkering with a company's systems and structures. Is the way people's performance is evaluated and rewarded consistent with the way you want them to think and act? Does the organization chart need to be redrawn to make it easier for people to work in new ways? Do you need to do something dramatic — like fire a few senior members of the old guard — to drive home the need for people to let go of old ways of doing things?

Doing things at this level is what's talked about in most books and videos and workshops on innovation, and it's not hard to find a few good ones. So I won't be talking about these things in this book. I'll focus instead on what you can do at the other level.

The operational level (what it is about)

At this level you are not concerned with innovation in general but with *making a specific one happen*. Managing innovation, here, means getting the resources needed to pursue a new idea, and motivating people to put in the effort required to implement it. Neither of these is an easy task.

Putting something new in place almost always requires more effort than doing a routine job. Things rarely go as expected, so they have to be re-worked. It's easy to underestimate how much time and effort you'll need to get the job done. Whatever your estimate you aren't likely to get all the resources you want. The same economic forces that push organizations to innovate also push them to run lean. In every case I know of, the people who've had to make an innovation happen have been stretched.

People usually have to find time for their innovation projects while still taking care of their regular jobs. The number of days in a week doesn't change to accomodate them.

Yes, people are sometimes assigned to a project full-time, but this doesn't exempt them from long hours. If you've ever managed one of these projects you know they tend to be under-staffed. They also have a high profile in the organization, which is a very mixed blessing. Nice for the egos of the people involved in it, especially at the beginning. Top management tells them how important their task is, how they are holding a piece of the organization's fate in their hands. And not to worry, they'll be given the time and resources they need to do it right. But soon after the project starts the pressure begins to build to deliver results quickly. People find that the pace at which they have to work and the hours they have to put in are similar to those needed to start a new business on a tight budget, the difference is they don't own any stock in the project.

Managing innovation at the operational level is a tough job. To do it successfully you have to create enthusiasm for the venture in several sets of people. Your own boss and subordinates, of course. But also people in other functions and departments, mostly your peers, sometimes people above and below them as well. This is because implementing something new in one area usually makes waves for and requires help from others. In this sense new ideas don't show much respect for organization charts.

Getting and motivating people to do what it takes to make an innovation happen is a tough job no matter where you work. Sure, it's easier to get permission to try new things in a place where the culture is innovation friendly than in one in which it is not. But in the former there are also likely to be more innovation projects going on, making it harder to get people to find time for yours.

What the Naturals Know How to Do

There are some people who have a knack for getting new ideas implemented, regardless of the kind of organization they're in. Of the more than ten thousand managers I've worked with, I'd say less than one in twenty have this knack. What do they know that the others don't?

They know how to tap sources of motivation that the others either don't know about or don't know how to tap. They understand that you can get to people's hearts through their minds. That what you do with people's ideas has a big impact on their motivation to help you do things. That if you engage people's minds in the right way you create goodwill toward you and toward your plans for making an innovation happen.

Most people know that you can increase others' commitment to a plan or decision by including their ideas in it. But they don't know how to make people their partners in thinking in a way that's productive and time effective. The one in twenty managers I'm talking about know how to do this. They also know how to do it in a way that enables them to gain far more commitment to a plan or decision than you get if all you do is give people a piece of ownership in it.

How these managers tap these sources of motivation is one of the best kept secrets around. No, they don't belong to some guild that jealously guards its know-how. How they do it is something most of them aren't clear about either. They are naturals. Which doesn't mean that they have a special ability that you and I don't have. It just means that they acquired their know-how largely unconsciously, through a process similar to the one we all use as kids to learn our native tongues. We can learn to speak them and even do that well, without being aware of the rules of grammar and syntax that we employ.

Anything they can do, you can do too

The "rules of engagement" described in this book are based on observations of what the "naturals" do. Using them will make you a more effective manager of innovation at the operational level. It will help you to get resources and motivate people to do the work needed to make specific innovations happen. It won't guarantee that you will be successful in doing these things in every situation, or with every person in it. But it will significantly raise your batting average.

If you are already a "natural," this book will increase your awareness of what you do and how you do it. And that will help you to do it more fully and consistently.

Here's how I learned about the "rules" described in this book.

The Surprising Lessons of Creativity Research — For Motivating People

I learned about the rules in a roundabout way. I studied physics and engineering and became the manager of product development for a company that made semiconductor devices. I left because I wanted to work for myself. I didn't have any set ideas about the kind of business I wanted to be in, as long as it was interesting. I happened to run into some people who were struggling to get off the ground a company based on what they had learned from their study of the creative process.

Their down to earth approach to the subject appealed to me. They recorded discussions of people trying to think of new ways to solve tough business problems. They then studied the tapes to see whether the people who had the most successful discussions thought about their problems differently than the others, who were equally expert in their fields. When they spotted what looked like a productive thinking habit they experimented with it to see if it consistently led to good results. If it did, they added it to their bag of tools. If not, they studied more tapes.

I liked this reliance on first-hand observation rather than on theories about the creative process. I also liked the focus on creativity as displayed not by Mozart or Picasso or Einstein, but by people like you and me thinking about everyday situations that required innovation. After working with them on a few projects I became a partner in the business.*

It took me a while to see the motivational impact of the "thinking tools" I was using in my work. I didn't get into the business because I was interested in the art and craft of motivating people. I was excited by the thought that you could put a handle on something as elusive as the creative process. I thought the main barrier to innovation was people's inability to think of good ideas, especially when pressured by time or other things. I didn't see that more often than not the problem was not a lack of ideas, but a failure to get others to buy into them.

And so I thought the sole purpose of the thinking habits we promoted was to help customers to tap the creative side of their minds. The measure of the effectiveness of our methods was the quality and quantity of the ideas they helped someone to produce, consistently and on demand. My attention was so focussed on this measure that I

---

* My partners were William J.J.Gordon, George M. Prince, and Cavas M. Gobhai. Bill developed the earliest version of the problem-solving process known as "synectics." That was also the name of the company that Bill and George started and that I had just joined.

didn't see that the kind of thinking that helped an individual to produce fresh ideas did something else as well *when two or more people
did that kind of thinking together. And this was that it increased their motivation to help each other get things done. It also eliminated a lot of friction
from their discussions.* But I had to be hit on the head several times
with these facts before they grabbed my attention.

The first hint was provided by the marketing manager of a division of a company that was one of our first customers. Ann could
extract something useful out of any old idea you gave her, no matter
how absurd or dumb sounding. Naturally we studied tapes of her
discussions to see how she did it. We also talked to her subordinates
to see if they knew. They didn't, but they talked about how much
they liked working for her. So, I thought, she's good with people too.
I didn't think this had anything to do with what she did with their
ideas.

I became convinced the two things were connected only after I
repeatedly saw things like this.

THE SITUATION

I run a meeting for the manager of a manufacturing
plant that is part of the European division of an American
company. The plant makes protective coatings and paints,
such as the ones used on ships to prevent corrosion and
the formation of barnacles. The purpose of the meeting is
to develop a plan for making the plant more profitable.

The people at the meeting are Paul, the plant manager,
four members of his staff, six non-plant people, and me.
Three of the six are scientists from the company's technology center in the U.S. The other three are marketing
people from the European division's head office.

We meet for dinner the night before the meeting. Keith,
one of the three scientists, makes it clear that though he
is pleased to have been invited to the meeting and hopes

to contribute some ideas that will help Paul and his team, he will not be able to give them more time anytime soon after this meeting. Maybe a day for a follow-up meeting in six months or so, but even that is not something they should count on. He has a lot of projects assigned to him, it's a struggle to find time for them all.

The other five non-plant people are quick to add that their situations are similar. They too will find it hard to give Paul more time than these few days.

In my pre-meeting discussions with Paul I told him that as the principal "owner" of the agenda he would have, at the end of the session, the final say over which of the ideas we developed would go into his action plan. But during the meeting he would have to be more than just an idea judge. To get the most out of people's ideas he would have to help them mold and modify their ideas to meet his requirements.

Paul did this in the session. He did an especially good job of extracting actionable ideas from the thoughts of the non-plant people who knew the least about the details of his plant's operation. And so something happened on the second day that pleased Paul even more than the useful ideas he was getting.

THE PLEASANT SURPRISE

We had spent the first day developing ideas for reducing the plant's operating costs. It's just before noon on the second day. We've been talking about products the plant could make that might be more profitable than the ones it is now making. We have a list of five candidates that appeal to everyone, including three that none of them has thought of before.

I ask Paul to outline the next steps that would need to be taken to pursue these ideas after the meeting, if they become part of the plan.

The thing that pleases Paul happens when he talks about what would need to be done with one of the three new ideas.

"We would want to talk to some customers," he says, "to get their reactions to the idea. And we would need to do some technical work to see if the product can be made the way we are thinking it can be made." He says that the latter is not something that could be done at the plant — it's work best done at the company's technology center in the U.S.

"If, at the end of the meeting, we decide that this is one of the ideas we should pursue," he says, "then I will submit a work request to Len."

Len is the director of the technology center.

"If you do that," says Keith, "it'll be six months at least before any work gets done on it. There are a lot of requests backed up on Len's desk, and this one will have to take its place in line. But Bill and I could do some unofficial work on it right away, don't you think Bill?"

"Well, that's right," says Bill, another of the scientists. "It's mostly a question of finding some technician time. It won't take you and me long to design the experiments we'd want them to run."

Paul gives me a quick look before he turns to Bill and Keith.

"That would be appreciated very much," he says.

Paul's look says to me that he's aware this is a big shift in the position Keith took — and others took with him — before the meeting. Which was: don't count on me to give you any more time after we're done here. Paul also noticed that Bill went along with Keith's shift. It becomes clear the next morning that the other four non-plant people have also changed their stance.

The last thing we do before the meeting ends is to outline a plan of action that includes a timetable and a listing of who is going to do what. Every one of the six non-plant people volunteers to do some of the work needed to implement the plan. The three people from the technology center pull out their calenders and I list on the flip-chart dates on which one or more of them are scheduled to be in Europe on other business. When Paul suggests it they all agree that it would be a good idea for the whole group to meet again in two months to review progress and, if necessary, to revise the action plan.

THE REST OF THE STORY

They met as planned two months later. All eleven of them didn't get together again as a group for another five months, but the smaller sub-teams they formed in the second meeting met several times. The group's efforts soon began to make a contribution to the plant's bottom line that was bigger than the increase Paul had told me he'd be pleased with.

I stopped being involved in the project after the second meeting. Two years after that meeting I ran into Keith in the U.S. when I was working on a different project for the company. I had not talked to Paul for about a year. I asked Keith if he knew how the plant was doing, and whether he was still doing anything related to the plan.

"Oh yes," he said, "I was there two weeks ago." He said that most of the work outlined in the action plan had been completed about six months ago, but one of the new product ideas had become a longer term technical project in which he and Bill were still involved. The two of them were the only ones of the six non-plant people who were still officially a part of the plant project, but the others kept in touch and were often used as a sounding board for ideas.

Key lesson: If you use people's heads in a good way, they'll let you borrow their hearts.

What motivated Keith and the others to give Paul, despite their busy schedules, far more of their time and energy than their initial idea of what they were prepared to give? What sustained, for close to two years, their high level of interest in helping Paul to implement his plan?

A sense of ownership — and a lot more

One thing that contributed to their motivation was, of course, that Paul's action plan was clearly *their* plan: they could see that their ideas, knowledge, and insights formed the threads of its fabric. The more ownership people feel they have in a plan or decision the more willing they are likely to be to help you move it forward. But a sense of ownership alone is rarely enough to elicit the kind of sustained effort people gave to Paul's project. To get it, you have to go beyond ownership, you have to tap additional sources of motivation.

Here's how the rules described in this book help you to tap these other sources.

■ You send people a powerful message

When you use the rules in your interactions with people you get good ideas from them. But in the process of getting these ideas you also send them a message: *I respect you, I value you.*

The message is powerful because it is believable. It's believable because you use the rules not to be nice to people but to get ideas and insights that are useful to you. Paul was persuaded to use the rules because he saw that they helped him to get good ideas for a project of some importance to him. It so happens that when you use the rules you get a happy by-product: you make a positive impact on people. To get to the good ideas he needed, Paul often had to work hard to extract useful ideas out of ones that, at first glance, seemed to have little or no value. When you find value in people's ideas you can't help making *them* feel valued. Each time you do this you add to the reservoir of their motivation to help you get things done.

■ You make working with you an affirming experience

The rules make it easy for you to draw on people's creativity.

11

Exercising their creativity in a productive way is an affirming experience, one that makes people feel good about themselves. If you enable people to have this experience you release a lot of goodwill toward you *and* toward the plan or decision for which you wanted their ideas.

■ You show them it's safe to trust you with their thoughts

Finally, the rules enable you to create a climate in which people feel it's safe to express thoughts they would normally keep to themselves, especially if you're the boss. For example, many people won't tell you what they think is wrong with your ideas if they feel this will upset you or make you defensive. And many will withhold ideas they have that they think aren't buttoned up. This means you don't get to hear most of the new thoughts that come into their heads when they are talking to you. New ideas rarely come to mind fully formed, so they are vulnerable to attack. To voice such ideas is to risk being ridiculed or thought impractical or even irresponsible.

If people feel that they can take such risks with you in a way that is not only safe but productive, then working with you becomes a positive experience. It's energizing to be around someone with whom you don't have to watch what you say because it might be held against you.

■ ■ ■ ■ ■

ABOUT THE RULES – A QUICK OVERVIEW

What's in this overview:

- A way to think about what the rules do for you.
- The two aspects of each rule.
- The reason for the order in which they are presented.

A way to think about what they do for you

The innovation process is like an organism that needs both fresh air and clean water to survive. If the air is good ideas, then the water is people's motivation to help you move the ideas forward.

The rules described in this book are like a dual pump that enables you to supply the process with both the "fresh air" and the "clean water." The way the rules do this is summarized in the diagram on the following page.

MOTIVATION
(to help you make an innovation happen)

- If you do the right thing with people's ideas you give them a sense of ownership in the project.
- You also tap other sources of motivation ...

... including the one you tap by enabling them to use their creativity in a productive way.

GOOD IDEAS

- All innovation starts with an idea for improving something.
- The process usually requires more good ideas along the way.
- Creative thinking is often needed to produce the ideas.

Rules for getting and processing people's ideas (and tapping their creativity).

CREATIVITY

INNOVATION

- Good ideas are rarely all you need to develop a successful new product or process. You also need to get others to approve the ideas and help you to implement them.
- The more an idea represents a departure from the current way of doing things, the harder it is to get others behind it (feels riskier to approvers, means more work for implementers).

A WAY TO THINK ABOUT WHAT THE RULES DO FOR YOU

The two aspects of each rule

To get good ideas and at the same time get people to want to help you make an innovation happen you need two things. One is awareness of the "how to" — knowing, for example, exactly what to do to get the most out of the ideas people give you, or how to tell when they have thoughts you need to draw out.

The second thing is the attitude or mindset without which you cannot profit from your knowledge of the "how to." An example of the required mindset is willingness to accept "idea help" from others.

You'll find that neither of these two things is complicated — neither the "how to" associated with any rule, nor what you can do to get into or maintain the necessary frame of mind. This doesn't mean it won't take a bit of effort to make doing these things second nature, something you do without having to think about how you do it — a la the naturals.

The reason for the order in which they are presented

The first two rules* are fundamental in a couple of ways. One is that you'll need to use the principles associated with them — frequently if not always — to get the full benefit from using any of the other rules. The second way in which the first two rules are basic is that they address the two biggest barriers to effective management of the people side of innovation. These are:

- lack of awareness of the mental process that produces good ideas,

  and

- the ego agenda that's present in all interactions because of the link between our ideas and our egos.

---

* Rule 1: Grow Ideas, Don't Mow Them Down
  Rule 2: Manage The Ego Agenda, Don't Let It Run The Show

Because the first two rules get you past these major barriers, you'll find that the increase in your effectiveness won't occur in a linear fashion — in eight equal steps as you make each rule a part of your habits of thought and interaction. It's likely that more than half the increase will come with the use of just the first two rules.

■ ■ ■ ■ ■

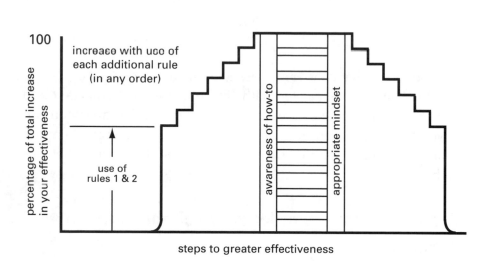

2

■ Rule 1: Grow Ideas, Don't Mow Them Down

Innovation is about doing something in a new or "better" way. The innovation process requires two kinds of ideas. One has to do with the "what" — the better product or procedure that you want to introduce. The other kind has to do with the "how" — your implementation plan.

As the person trying to make an innovation happen your role is similar to that of an orchestra or jazz band leader. What you're leading is more like a symphony orchestra if the "what" is relatively fixed, and there's room for people's ideas primarily in the "how." It's more like a jazz band if there's flexibility in both areas. In either case, you need to create as much room as possible for the ideas of your "band" or team.* You want room for their ideas because, if you get these the right way, you will both improve the quality of your ideas and increase people's motivation to help you implement them.

It's not hard to include people's ideas in the "what" or the "how" if you think the ideas are good ones. It's a challenge to do this when you *don't* think they're any good.

---

* By "team" I mean anyone — boss, peer, subordinate, customer, or supplier — whose help you need to make an innovation happen. I *don't* mean only those people who report to you or are officially assigned to your project.

The Qualities That Make an Idea "Good"

By "good" ideas I mean those that meet three criteria. One, they are *practical*. Which means that they are doable given your time and resource constraints, and that you can pursue them without getting into any trouble you don't want to get into. But you won't want to include them in your plan if they don't appear to improve it in some way, to add *edge* to it — either by giving you a piece that was needed but missing from it, or by giving you a way to do something that's better than the one you have.

The third thing a "good" idea has is *appeal*. If you — and others in your team — don't feel positively about it, you're likely to either ignore it or, if you do something with it, to not give it your best effort.

The thing that makes it hard to get to people's hearts through their minds is that most of the ideas they give you are likely to be ones you think are *not* good. I've asked a lot of managers what percentage of the ideas they get from others could be called good, as defined — they're practical, *and* they give you an edge you didn't have, *and* your reaction is "I like it!" I haven't kept a precise count of the answers, but if I had and put the answers on a chart it would look something like this:

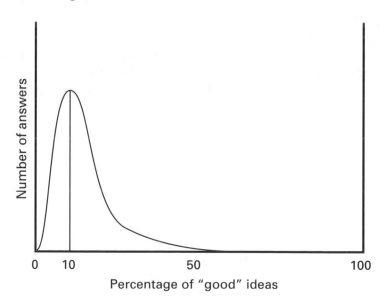

Most people's answers cluster around ten percent. More say "one percent" than say "twenty." A number over fifty is rarely mentioned.

And what do you do, I ask people, with the ideas you get that you think are *not* good? Here's what one group of managers said.

"Well, you reject them," says Kevin.

"You shoot them down," says Ed. "Unless they belong to your boss. Then you get someone else to do it."

"Sometimes they get built on," says Lizette.

"Not in any meetings I've been in lately," says Kevin.

"If you think of an idea that's got a lot of holes in it, you keep it to yourself," says Dan. "Better to kill it yourself than to have others do it for you."

"Now we know what kinds of ideas *he* has," says Ed.

People in different parts of the world use different words, but their answers are essentially the same. In most groups there are one or two people who say that if you're given an idea that is impractical or flawed in some other way, you should build on it. But few of the ones who say this actually do it when the ideas are about a situation that matters to them. When this is the case they do what everyone else does — ignore the ideas or reject them.

Why the Response That Seems Reasonable Is Often Not the One to Make

Turning away from or trying to kill what looks like a bad idea is such a universal response that I think it's the mental kin of the physical flight or fight response that's built into our systems. The first thing that comes to mind is all the grizzly bears we could run into if we did the thing suggested.

So what we do with ideas is to screen them — to do a quick evaluation of them, label them "good" or "bad," then keep the first kind and discard the second. The most common reason for rejecting ideas is that they lack practicality. For whatever reason we do this, it seems like a reasonable thing to do. Why waste time and energy on bad ideas, other than to find a nice way to say no?

19

"Screening" is indeed the right thing to do if you are on the brink of action and are being asked to decide, right then, which ideas to go forward with and which not. But it's *not* the thing to do if you aren't done thinking and are looking for good ideas. Here's why.

Good ideas are the end-product of a process of evolution that usually starts with ideas that are flawed — often seriously

If you could videotape and then watch replays of what happens in your head when it produces good ideas, you'd see that most of them had very humble beginnings. I haven't put a camera in anyone's head, but I have filmed hundreds of groups talking about a wide range of problems and opportunities for which they wanted good ideas. What I saw on these tapes isn't any different from what's known to people — such as writers and inventors — who are both creative and self-observant. Here's what one such person said about how he got one of his ideas.

Edwin Land, the inventor of the Polaroid camera, described how he got the idea for it. He was at home one day taking pictures with a conventional camera. His little daughter wanted to see the pictures right away. You know how kids can be. "I want to see them now," she said, "why can't I?"

So Land explained to her, as best he could to a child, why not. The film in the camera could be hurt by light, so you couldn't take it out and look at it until it had been treated in a special way, after which it wasn't bothered by light. This could only be done in a dark-room that had in it all the things needed for the treatment. They didn't have such a room so the film, carefully wrapped, had to be sent to a place that had one. The people there fixed the film and made it into pictures and sent them back. All this took time.

"And that's that," he found himself saying, "unless I could put that darkroom in the camera for you."

He was just joking but his daughter didn't know that.

"Oh Daddy, I like that idea," she said, "why can't we do it?"

Most people would have told her that it wasn't practical and tried to explain why not. But Land was an inventor. He didn't say, in effect, "let me help you to grow up my dear, here's why in the real world you can't do that." Instead he said "That's a very good question, let me think about it."

He said he then went for a long walk. It was during that walk that he saw how it might be practical to do inside a camera what was being done in the darkroom. To see this he needed to know a little chemistry and physics, but this knowledge would have been more of a hindrance than a help without his willingness to give some serious thought to an idea that began life as a joke.

Good ideas seldom come to you fully formed and nicely gift wrapped

The ideas you get most of the time are like raw material that you have to work with and re-shape to get out of it something you can use. There are two reasons for this:

- *One has to do with the nature of the creative side of the mind. Its function seems to be to produce raw material and not finished product. What's usually missing in this material is practicality. I'd be willing to bet that if you could talk to your creative side it would say "Practicality? I don't do that, it's not part of my job description. My job is to give you ideas that are new or different from the way you've been thinking about things. You add the practicality."*

- *If the idea that's new to you comes from another person, there's a second reason why it's seldom something you can buy and take home as is. The idea may not be raw material in the sense that it is something that just occurred to the other person. That person may have already done a lot of work on it before presenting it to you. But ideas that represent a finished product to others are like their clothes — they are seldom made to fit your measurements and preferences. So they have to be altered before you can wear them comfortably. And perhaps re-dyed so you want to wear them.*

21

Contrary to the popular notion, good ideas are not born fully formed in a flash of light. The sense of a light bulb going on usually comes from the sudden coming together of bits and pieces of thought into a concrete or finished form. The bits and pieces, and the coming together of them, are the products of a kind of thinking that's very different from the one required to screen ideas — that is, to evaluate and label them "good" or "bad."

In this other way of thinking there is no such thing as a good or bad idea, only raw material — like ore or seeds — that can't be judged by the same criteria as finished product. Ideas, in this way of thinking, can also be likened to children or babies who could become adults with any of a number of capabilities, depending on the kind of guidance and nourishment they were given. You wouldn't give a job interview to a six-month-old baby — you don't know whether it's going to grow up to be a good or bad doctor or plumber or architect. It's just as inappropriate to make final judgements about the value of a "baby" idea, which is how you have to think of people's ideas if you want to get the most out of them.

GETTING THE MOST OUT OF IDEAS – THINGS TO KEEP IN MIND

- Most of the ideas you get from people are likely to be ones you think are *not* good. This doesn't mean there's nothing of value in them.

- What makes it hard to get the most out of people's ideas is the tendency to screen them, even when that's not the thing to do.

- Good ideas rarely come to you fully formed and nicely gift wrapped. You have to fashion them out of the raw material you're given. There are two reasons for this:

  - the job of the creative side of the mind is to give you ideas that are fresh and different — it is not concerned with practicality;

   - other people's thought-through ideas are like their
     clothes — made mostly to their measurements and
     preferences, not yours ... to be able to wear them
     you usually have to alter them.

 • The above are the reasons why — if you look carefully
   at the ideas you get from people — you'll find that, as
   given:

   - if they're new or different, they're usually not accept-
     able;

   - if they're acceptable, they're usually not different or
     new.

The Idea Growing Process

How do you convert raw material into finished product? How do you "grow" an idea?

The process is simple, almost obvious once you stop to think about it. You look at the pros and cons of what you've been given, and then you think of ways to change the idea so you keep its plusses but not its flaws. What could be simpler?

But though the concept is straightforward, making it work for you usually requires you to get past one or more mental barriers. And you have to exercise your imagination.

The example that follows illustrates these things. It also illustrates something else. And this is that:

The more negative your initial reaction to an idea, the more likely it is to contain in it the seeds of the good idea you need.

THE SITUATION

Steve, one of the owners of a small business, is meeting with his two partners, Byron and Dave. Their company makes a family of electrical devices used in controls for industrial equipment.

This is one of their monthly business meetings. The agenda item they've just begun to discuss is the network of distributors through whom they sell their products. The network was carefully built up over the years and for the most part this way of doing business works well, both for the company and for its ultimate customers. But Byron, the partner responsible for both product development and manufacturing, feels that the arrangement sometimes keeps them from responding quickly to their end-user's needs. He thinks there's room here for some innovation.

The network is Steve's baby. He is the partner in charge of sales, and he has worked hard to find the right distributors — and to develop the working relationships with them that are essential to the smooth operation of the network. He is understandably sensitive to any criticism of it. But he has done a good job of staying cool and listening to Byron's concerns about it.

THE RAW MATERIAL

Byron is done with his comments about the network. There's a brief pause, and then Steve says:

"Yeah, well I'm open to any suggestions you guys have for how we could improve our distribution system."

Another pause and then Dave, the partner who looks after their finances, says "O.K., here's an off-the-wall idea. Why don't we get rid of the distributors and go direct to the customer. We could do it without adding a lot of people to our payroll, we could create a sales force of reps who work for us on a commission basis."

Byron looks at Dave and then at Steve. He can't imagine Steve having much use for the idea. Steve says to Dave:

"Do you want me to respond to that seriously?"

Dave says "I have to admit I threw that in just to shake up both of you a little, but now that it's out there it wouldn't hurt to talk about it."

Steve looks at Byron, who says, "You call it, Steve."

Steve scratches the back of his neck and says "I guess you're right, Dave, it can't hurt to talk about the idea. O.K., give me a minute to think about it."

He gets up, picks up his coffee cup, and goes to the big window that takes up most of one wall of the room. He stands there for a while looking out over the company parking lot.

"I'll be darned," he says finally as he turns around.

THE MENTAL BARRIERS

I have a guess about what just happened in Steve's head. He was in one of my workshops, and knows about growing ideas. I'm present because he sold his partners on the idea of having me sit in on a few of their meetings and comment afterwards on their problem-solving process. I'll be doing that at the end of the meeting.

When an idea represents a big change from the way you've been running your business — or your life — the first thing that usually comes to mind is all the reasons why it's a bad idea. This is especially the case if it's an approach you considered taking at one time but rejected in favor of the one you are now using. I'm guessing Steve has in the past thought of doing something similar to what Dave has suggested, probably before Dave joined the company two years ago.

| The first barrier |

The first thing you have to do to grow an idea you don't like is to get past your initial negative reaction to it. This is because as long as the idea's flaws are in the front of your mind they block your vision and you can't see its other side, which is its potential advantages — what you might gain by doing something like it. These potential advantages are the seeds of the good idea that may be contained in the bad one you've been given. Without these seeds you haven't got anything to grow.

You fight thoughts with other thoughts. You can get past your negative reaction by reminding yourself that you are engaged in ideation, not decision-making. And therefore your purpose in giving the idea more thought is not to try to talk yourself into liking it as it stands, but to see if it can be changed into something you could like.

A short-hand way of reminding yourself of all this is to put the idea in quotes — "... get rid of the distributors..." The quotes say that you don't have to take the idea literally because you don't know what it's going to look like when you're done with it. It's a work in progress. This reminder will help move the thoughts of the idea's flaws back far enough to unblock your vision. And then you can see its other side.

You'll then find that in most cases one or two potential benefits of the idea come to mind easily. These are usually the obvious ones. But these rarely supply the fuel needed by the imagination to change the ugly lump of ore you've been given into a piece of gold you can use. The needed fuel comes from the non-obvious plusses of the idea.

Second barrier

It takes a bit of effort to think beyond the obvious at any time. In the idea growing process the task is made harder because it's just at this point that the mind tends to shift its focus back to the idea's flaws, and to get discouraged by the thought of them.

At this point it's critical to be patient with yourself. Give yourself a little time to think. It helps to remember the quotation marks. The key is to take your time. Ten seconds is often enough; you seldom need more than a minute. This is what I thought Steve was doing when he went to stand by the window.

You know you've found a non-obvious plus if you feel a bit surprised by it — it's something you hadn't expected to find in the idea. And then, nineteen times out of twenty, it isn't long before the good idea begins to take shape in your mind. This is what I think has happened to Steve when he turns from the window and says "I'll be darned."

WHAT THE IDEA BECOMES

"We always talk," Steve goes on to say, "about the need to segment our ultimate customers, to recognize that they don't all have the same requirements, and that therefore we have to approach different groups of them differently. But I never thought of doing the same thing with our distributors, until I started to wrestle with Dave's idea. I think I see where to go with it."

"Don't tell me you've talked yourself into doing what he suggested, getting rid of our distribution network," says Byron. "I know I have some complaints about it, but it's not something I'd want us to do away with."

"I wouldn't either," Steve says. "If we did that we'd quickly lose a big chunk of our share of the market, a share we might never get back. But not to worry, that's not what I'm about to propose. The best way to tell you what that is may be to tell you how I got there."

"Because of all the red flags it raised I had to keep telling myself that I wasn't being asked to decide whether or not to do exactly what Dave suggested, just to think about what we might gain *if* we were to do it.

He says a couple of benefits came to mind.

"The first thought," he says, "was that going direct to customers would shorten our lines of communication with them, and then we would learn about and could respond more quickly to changes in their needs. Which is what you, Byron, would like to do."

"Another plus was that it would be easier for customers to get nonstandard products from us. We know our distributors like to push our standard lines. They discourage inquiries about specials because these involve small quantities, so the business is less profitable for them. But that business can be very profitable for us."

And then, he says, he got a bit stuck.

"I couldn't think of any more plusses," he says, "at least not right away. My mind went blank for a while, couldn't have been for more than a few seconds but it felt a lot longer. And then I saw that if you take the idea to mean not doing away with our network but weaving some direct-to-the-customer paths into it, then there could be a plus in it *for our distributors.* We could free them from having to do the small quantity business most of them don't like to do."

This made him think that there were also some customers that many distributors didn't like to work with.

"Mostly these are the design and development departments of the big equipment makers. Again, these departments order only small quantities of our products. And they want a lot of technical information. Giving these customers the time and attention they want is good for us all in the long term, but it's easier for some distributors to make that investment than it is for others."

Byron says "There are also distributors who do fine with our established products but don't do a good job with our new ones. They are good order takers, they are good at delivering to our customers on time. But selling is not their strong point, and new products have to be sold."

"That's right," says Steve. He gets up again, goes to the table with the coffee pot on it, and refills his cup. He looks at Byron.

"So what do you think of this," he says. "We go out and talk to our distributors, get them to help us identify situations in which it would benefit us all if we worked directly with the customer. In some cases this could be only when the customer is not done developing a new line of equipment, when it goes into production we hand the account back to the distributor. Maybe an arrangement like that also for our nonstandard and new products."

He pauses.

"We'd have to figure out how to manage the handoffs from us to them in a way that is painless for the customer," he says. "And there's probably other things we need to work out, but I think the distributors will go for it. We're always telling them what they could be doing to give better service to the customer, but we've never sat down with them and asked what *we* could be doing to make *their* job easier.

"I like it," Byron says. "I think we should try it out on a small scale first, maybe for a couple of customers and one of our new products. See how it works and what it will take by way of resources before we go all out with it."

"Yes, of course," says Steve, "that's what I was thinking too."

"Makes me more comfortable with it too," Dave says, "if we're talking about doing a pilot to test the idea before we make big changes in the way we do business. The fact that we're doing a reasonably good job of it doesn't mean we shouldn't make changes, but let's do that carefully."

"You said it," says Steve.

■ ■ ■ ■ ■

The parts of the process, and the two ways of growing ideas

The idea growing process can be divided into two parts. The first is an appraisal of the raw material in front of you. But it's an appraisal with a difference. You don't just do a quick analysis of an idea's pros and cons, you use your creativity to explore its possibilities. This is what you do when you stretch to find its non-obvious plusses. Doing this makes it *an appraisal that adds value.* If you do a good job of this, the second part of the process usually goes easily and well.

The second part is the one in which you actually grow the idea by thinking of ways to keep its potential advantages but not its drawbacks. In doing this you *change the idea.* You can do this in one of two very different ways: you can *tailor* the idea, or you can *transform* it.

You tailor an idea if you actually want to do some or all of what is being suggested, but have some concerns about doing it. Steve wanted to do the "go direct to the customer" part of Dave's idea, but not in any way that would make them lose market share.

Tailoring involves subtracting bits from an idea, or adding bits to it, or otherwise *modifying* it. Steve's modifications included going direct to the customer only in certain circumstances, and in a way that enhanced the existing system instead of doing away with it. The modifications you make can be minor or major, but some part of the idea stays recognizably the same.

You transform an idea when you either can't or don't want to take it literally, you want to think of it as a figure of speech. You transform an idea by thinking of a completely different way of going after one or more of the plusses of the idea. The transformed idea usually bears as little resemblance to the original idea as a butterfly does to the caterpillar it once was. When you transform an idea you don't modify it, you *metamorphose** it. Here's an example of what I mean.

* metamorphosis: a complete change of form, structure, or substance.

THE SITUATION

Beth is an architect who works for a large firm. Outside this job she is a member of a small group of volunteers dedicated to the task of helping people in crumbling sections of the city to rejuvenate their neighborhoods. I'm working with Beth and three others of this group. They are talking about a problem they're having in one such neighborhood, in which Beth is the leader of the project.

Beth reviews the problem. She is finding it difficult to get things going because the people in this section of the city seem particularly indifferent to their surroundings.

"We need to do something to get them to care," she says. "We can help them get money and provide expertise but they are the ones who have to do the rebuilding and the long term maintenance. And it's a lot easier for us to get local and state funding for the project if there is strong community support for it."

Beth's group has approached the community through the local church. The minister and several members of the congregation have become strong allies and are working with them to get the rest of the community involved in the project. They have taken Beth and others of her group to visit people in their homes, and have helped organize town hall-style meetings at the church. But so far they have not been able to stimulate a lot of interest.

"We need to do something different," Beth says.

■ ■ ■ ■ ■

The thinking that gets you to a good idea is like a three-stage rocket. It requires three bursts of creativity. The first stage is the one that produces the raw material. (This is what "brainstorming" does.) The second stage is the one needed to find non-obvious plusses, and the third burst of creativity is needed to power the last part of the process — the tailoring and transforming of ideas.

The easiest way to stimulate production of fresh ideas in the first stage is to ask for ideas that *must not be practical.* This invites the creative side of the mind to go to work. Beth knows this.

THE IDEA

"How about some ideas," Beth says to the others, "that are so impractical that surely I wouldn't have thought of trying them."

After a brief silence Fred says "How about this. Go out and capture the biggest rats you can find. Bring 'em back to the neighborhood and let 'em loose on a weekend when everyone is around. That ought to shake people out of their apathy."

Beth blinks and gives Fred a wry look. Everyone else laughs.

"Don't think we're going to top that one," someone says to Beth, "why don't we just go with it.

"Want to make sure there aren't any other ideas people want to throw out before we work on that one," Beth says and looks around.

No others are offered. "O.K.," Beth says, "I did ask for it."

She stares at the floor for a few seconds.

31

"Rats," she says without looking up. "They make me think of disease. O.K., so maybe if we did this it would raise people's awareness of unsanitary conditions in the neighborhood, things that need to be cleaned up."

Another pause. She looks up at the person who is noting her plusses on a flip-chart.

"When I was a child," she says, "I was terrified of rats. I thought if I ever ran into one it would attack me. Which suggests that perhaps we would make people worry about their kids getting bitten, and worries about your children's safety can be a powerful motivator."

A longer pause. Then she sits up a little in her chair.

"Well," she says, "if the rats were big enough we'd make the evening news. It wouldn't be very positive publicity, but we'd get the attention of the media."

"Good one," says the person at the flip-chart.

Beth looks around at the group. "I'm sure you can guess what I think is wrong with this idea and why I'm not taking it literally. So my question to us is how do we keep these plusses without using rats? What could we do to heighten awareness of unsafe conditions? How can we tap into people's concerns for their kids? How could we get the media to give the project and the community some publicity — positive, not negative?"

In about ten minutes Beth and the group arrive at an idea that she likes a lot. It is built around the concept of getting people to care by linking the project to their hopes and concerns for their children. The idea of letting rats loose in the neighborhood is transformed into a project kick-off event whose centerpiece would be an exhibit of drawings, photographs, and videos made by young people in the community. They would be asked to try to capture the essence of the things about their current physical environment that troubled them the most, as well as the things about it that they would most like to preserve.

Beth says she can see how a lot of unsafe conditions could be translated into strong images — children playing in abandoned lots threading their way through the broken glass of discarded windows and other dangerous junk; toddlers with their hands to their mouths with peeling lead paint in the background; unlit areas and empty houses that provided sanctuary to pushers from outside the community.

"We don't have to stage any of this," she says, "it's all there. And I've met young people who are interested in photography and film-making. I think I could go to one of the local T.V. stations, and to a newspaper, and get them to loan us some equipment. And if they do that, they'll want to cover the event."

Over lunch break Beth was able to reach a couple of her contacts in the community and discuss the idea with them.

"They both agreed," she tells us, "that if we go about it the right way this thing has the potential to get the community more solidly behind us."

■ ■ ■ ■ ■

The two preceding stories illustrate the two different ways in which you can grow ideas. They both illustrate another aspect of the process. And this is that:

It's easier to add practicality to an idea that's fresh but flawed, than it is to add freshness to one that's practical but old and tired.

A RULE 1 COROLLARY: DRIVE FOR GOOD IDEAS, BUT DON'T GET TOO ATTACHED TO ANY ONE OF THEM

The most immediate and tangible products of the idea growing process are the good ideas you get out of it. This, coupled with the fact that good ideas have a way of grabbing the imagination, can make you forget that when you involve other people in the process the ideas are not the only — or even the most important — things you get from it.

It is of course important that you get out of the process some ideas you like. They are proof that you found the discussion productive. Most people, especially those who like to think they are task-oriented, need some hard evidence to convince themselves that they made a useful contribution to your thinking, and that they can go ahead and let themselves feel good about that. But seeing that you got useful ideas from it isn't the only thing that makes the discussion with you a positive experience for them.

When you grow people's ideas you show them that you can be trusted with concepts that aren't all buttoned up, and that are therefore vulnerable to attack. They see that you add value to the raw material they give you, you don't trash it. And you give them an opportunity to exercise their imagination and creativity.

All these things make people want to be on your team, to help you get things done. This goodwill towards the specific tasks you discuss with them, and towards working with you in general, is a less tangible product of the process than the ideas you get out of it. But it is just as real, and in many cases the more important of the two outcomes.

Remember, the innovation process is like an organism that needs both "fresh air" (good ideas) and "clean water" (people's motivation to help you get things done). And that more often than not what the organism doesn't get enough of is not the fresh air but the clean water.

■ ■ ■ ■ ■

In Steve's case the idea of weaving direct-to-the-customer paths into his distribution network emerged from a discussion with his partners. The way he got it will incline them to help him move it forward, and he will need this help if he wants to see it implemented successfuly.

But he is also going to need the help of his distributors. The odds of getting it will be greatly increased if he incorporates elements of their thinking into his final plan of action. If he does this right he will not only give them a sense of ownership in it, he will also tap additional sources of goodwill.

The concept he and his partners developed needs to be fleshed out so there is room in it for distributor's ideas. But if their support is a key to achieving the objectives of the approach, then Steve needs to stay open to any *different* approaches that may emerge from his discussions with them, even if this means letting go of the idea he and his partners developed. Of course if he does this he will have to get Byron and Dave to buy into the alternative approach, but this will not be difficult, for two reasons:

- *First, it is more important for his partners to have a sense of ownership in the* objectives *the plan is designed to accomplish than in the specific means used to do that. Byron knows that it's the issues he raised that will drive any plan Steve decides to implement. Both Byron and Dave also know that he will heed their wish to test the plan with a pilot effort before committing the company to it.*

- *The second reason it will not be hard to get their backing for an alternative approach is that the rules of engagement he has been using in his interactions with them have created a reservoir of goodwill that he can draw on.*

■ ■ ■ ■ ■

In Beth's case she needs to involve in the idea development

process the other set of "owners" of the problem — key members of the community. She took a first step toward doing this by bouncing the idea off a couple of them. A lot of the details of how to implement the concept remain to be worked out, so in her case also there's room for other's ideas. But Beth will also need to be ready to let the idea go if these other "owners" come up with ones that are different.

■ ■ ■ ■ ■

In many situations there is more than one good way to accomplish something. This is especially true for people problems, though even for technical ones there is rarely only one good answer. But it isn't always easy to stay open to other ideas after you've developed one you like, especially if it's one — as was Beth's — whose production required a creative act of transformation. When you are a part of that act you feel as if you had just pulled a rabbit out of a hat, and it's easy to get attached to the critter. You can counter this attachment by keeping in mind two things:

- *When the quality of the help you get from others is a key to achieving results and when there's more than one acceptable way to go, what makes one way better than the other is not its objective merits but its appeal to the people whose help you need.*

- *If you know how to grow ideas you can always find another good one, so you can afford to let a few go.*

GROWING IDEAS – USING THE PRINCIPLES

What's in this section:

- A Quick Review Summary
- A Practice Note.

QUICK REVIEW SUMMARY

Reading the previous chapter once may be all you need to do to start growing ideas more consistently, easily, and skillfully than you did before you read it. If you're like most people, you may also need to review the principles involved from time to time, especially before the first few times you consciously practice the rule.

What follows is a "Quick Review" summary of the why and how of growing ideas.

The Why

- Most of the ideas others give you are likely to be *not* good. ("Good" ones are not only *practical,* they also give you an *edge* you didn't have, *and* they have *appeal.*) But because the ideas aren't good doesn't mean they don't contain in them the seeds of ones you can use.

- What makes it hard to find value in most ideas is the habit of screening them — of quickly labelling them "good" or "bad" and then getting rid of the latter.

Screening is the right thing to do if you have to decide, right then, whether or not to implement an idea pretty much as it stands.

Screening is *not* the thing to do if you aren't done thinking, and you are looking for good ideas.

- Good ideas are the end-product of a process of evolution that

37

usually starts with ideas that are flawed ... often seriously.

- If you want to get the most out of the ideas you're given, it helps to think of them as raw material and not finished product to which you have to say either "yes" or "no." There are two reasons why the ideas you get may be "unfinished" and therefore not acceptable as candidates for action:

  - If an idea is new — that is, it's something you or another person just thought of — then it's likely to lack practicality (that's how the creative side works).

  - If it's someone else's idea and that person *has* done some growing before presenting it to you, it may still be unacceptable to you because its development was guided by the other person's wishes and concerns, not yours — and your's are different.

- Good ideas aren't the only — or often even the most important — thing you get from the process. By extracting useful ideas from the raw material you get from others, you also increase their motivation to help you get things done. You do this in two ways: by giving them a sense of ownership in your plans, and by making them feel valued and respected.

The How

As you read the following review of the idea growing process, keep in mind that the key to using it successfully is not strict adherence to the steps outlined below. You can play jazz with these. The key is to be aware of the mental blocks you're likely to encounter, and to make the guidelines for getting past them a part of your thinking habits.

The idea growing process

The process has two parts. In the first you do an assay of the idea, and decide how you want to grow it. In the second part you do the growing.

Part A: Appraisal that adds value

1. Find the "seeds" (what's going for the idea?)

a) *Put the idea in quotes ("...")*

What can make it hard to see what is going for an idea is thoughts about its flaws.

Given an unacceptable idea, the first thing that usually comes to mind is what's wrong with it. This can make your practical side anxious. If that happens your attention can get so focussed on the flaws that you can't see anything else.

You can unblock your vision by reminding your practical side that you are not about to say "yes" to the idea as it stands. It's just raw material. When you're done growing it the finished product may look very different. And in the process you are going to fix its flaws, you're not going to forget about them.

A short-hand way of saying all this is to mentally put quotation marks around the concept, meaning you don't need to take the idea literally because it's going to change.

b) *Identify "3–5" potential advantages (including 1–2 that are non-obvious)*

The reason for the "3–5" is this. A couple of plusses usually come to mind easily, but these tend to be ones that are obvious. Going for more than two will, in most cases, ensure that you dig out at least one that is *not* obvious. (If three come easily, go for four or more. The principle is: at least one more than come easy.)

Thinking of at least one non-*obvious plus is important because it is these that:*

- provide the kind of "seeds" that make the end-product one that has "edge" and "appeal" in addition to practicality;

- make your appraisal of the idea one that adds value to it.

You know you've found a non-obvious plus when you feel a bit surprised by it — it's something you hadn't expected to find in the idea.

Key: Give yourself some quiet, unhurried time to think.

(Finding non-obvious plusses requires creative thinking, and you can't hurry your creative side. Ten seconds will usually do it, you seldom need as much as a minute.)

2. Decide how you want to grow the idea

Time now to focus on what's wrong with the idea, and on how you want to change it.

The thing to watch for here is the tendency to think of the idea's flaws as counterweights to the plusses you've just identified. If you do that you'll slide out of the growing and into the screening mode of thought. In the latter mode it's O.K. to weigh the pros against the cons so you can make a "yes" or "no" decision about the idea, but that's not what you need to do here.

In the grow mode, the flaws are used to decide how and in which direction you want to grow the idea.

a) Identify the flaw(s) (up to 3, if necessary)

All you need to do here is to identify the biggest flaw, but this isn't always the first one that comes to mind. Sometimes you have to think of a couple — rarely more than three — to see clearly which of them is most important to you.

You don't need a complete inventory of the flaws because in the process of fixing the big one you are going to change the idea. When you do that you will often eliminate other flaws as well, but it's hard to know which ones. For this reason it's best to *work on the flaws one at a time.* Take care of the big one, then see what remains to be done.

b) *Select the fork you want to take (tailor or transform?)*

You *tailor* if you actually want to do some or all of what is being suggested, but have concerns about doing it. To take care of your concerns you *modify* the idea. (By adding or subtracting bits, or by changing how or in what circumstances you would implement it.)

You *transform* an idea when you can't or don't want to take it literally (e.g., Get close to your customers by "adopting their kids,"). When you transform an idea you *metamorphose* it. (By thinking of a *different** way to go after one or more of the plusses of the initial idea.)

c) **Pose the right question**

To grow the idea into something that you will find acceptable, you need to focus people's thinking on the right question.

If tailoring

The generic question is, of course, how to eliminate the biggest problem you see with doing some or all of what's been suggested. But you may need to be more specific if there is more than one direction in which you could look for answers to this question.

For example, say your top concern about an idea is that it would take a lot of time to implement it. What's the question you want answered? How to find the time? How to justify it? How to modify the idea so it won't need as much time?

Sometimes the direction in which you want to look for answers is obvious. People may know you'll need your boss's permission to spend time on the idea, and that you want them to think about how to justify that.

But often it is *not* obvious in which direction you want to grow an idea. You can make it clear by posing the right question.

(It's especially important to focus people's thinking on the right question when you give them your appraisal of an idea but don't go on to grow it

---

* It can be as different as a butterfly is from the caterpillar it once was.

right then — instead, you ask them to go think of ways to modify it. You don't want them coming back with answers to the wrong question.)

If transforming

The generic question here is "how to attain some or all of the plusses of the idea in a *different,* more practical way."

When you want people to transform an idea, you want them to be free to change it so completely that it bears no resemblance to the original. For this reason you *don't* want to restrict their thinking by posing a more specific question — though you may want to word the generic one differently in different situations. (For example, in Beth's case, "how to get the same results without using rats.")

Part B: Tailoring or Transforming

Just one step here — you tailor or transform the idea as per the question(s) you pose in Part A.

If you tailor: You may need to modify the idea more than once — the first time to take care of the big flaw, then to fix remaining ones.

But if after several modifications you still don't have an acceptable idea, it's often because you are trying to tailor an idea that needs to be transformed. So back up and take the other fork.

If you transform: After you transform an idea, you may also need to tailor it a bit to make it fully acceptable. (You've turned the caterpillar into a butterfly, but the wings need more color.)

Two things to keep in mind:
- *Watch for the tendency, in Part B, to sit back and expect others — especially the person whose idea it is — to fix its flaws. The odds of changing it into something acceptable to you are greatly increased if you stay actively engaged in the process.*

- *Watch also for the tendency to keep thinking of an idea as it was given to you, to imprison it in that form — to "set it in stone."*

  The key to finding ideas you can use is to let the ones in front of you change into something different.

THE IDEA GROWING PROCESS: AT-A-GLANCE SUMMARY

Part A: Appraisal that adds value

1. *Find the "seeds" (what's going for the idea?)*
   a) Put the idea in quotes (". . .")
   b) Identify "3–5" potential advantages (dig for 1–2 that are non-obvious.)

   Key: give yourself time to think.

2. *Decide how you want to grow the idea*
   a) Identify the flaw(s) (up to 3, if necessary)
   b) Select the fork you want to take (tailor or transform?)
   c) Pose the right question.

   Example of c): if you want to tailor and the big flaw is high cost, is the question how to justify it? How to reduce cost? Other?

Part B: Tailoring or Transforming

Just one step here — tailor or transform as per the question(s) you pose in Part A.

To tailor: modify (by adding or subtracting bits, or by changing the manner or circumstances in which you pursue the idea).
To transform: metamorphose (by thinking of a *different* way of going after one or more plusses of the initial idea).

Things to keep in mind:
- *If after several "tailorings" you still don't have an acceptable idea, back up and take the other fork (transform the idea).*
- *Be actively engaged in the process, don't sit back and wait for others to fix the flaws for you.*
- *Let the idea change, don't "set it in stone."*

PRACTICE NOTE

Though it's a natural way of thinking, most people don't use the muscles of the mind required to grow ideas as much as they use those needed to screen them — to quickly evaluate and label them "good" or "bad." The muscles needed to do the one kind of thinking are therefore weaker than those needed for the other. The stronger ones tend to take over when you feel rushed or pressured, and then you can find yourself screening ideas even when you know it's not the productive thing to do.

If you find this happening, you may want to do the equivalent of the finger exercises that piano players — and other musicians — do to make the muscles of their hands supple and strong. (If you do this, you'll find that it takes a lot less time to keep the muscles of the mind in shape than it takes to do the same thing for those of your body.)

Here's a five-minute exercise you can do, by yourself, whenever you have the time.

Take a moment to recall a few ideas that you recently rejected (out loud or in your mind). Select one of them and grow it.

If it helps, use the At-A-Glance summary of the process as a guide.

Other things that will help:

• Do the exercise when you aren't feeling rushed.

• Put your thoughts on paper (if you aren't in the shower, or driving, or doing something else that precludes it). Write down the plusses, the flaw(s), the question(s) you pose to yourself, and your thoughts about how the idea could be changed. This will help in two ways:

  - having to put your thoughts into words clarifies them;

- it's easier to do the thinking you need to do in one step if you don't have to worry about losing the thoughts you had in a previous step.

• Try to get out of the exercise an idea you can use, but don't make this your primary objective. It's more important to attend to the process.

Be aware of the step you're in, and notice which part of it goes easily and which part not so easily. (The latter is where you need to spend more practice time.)

3

■ Rule 2: Manage the Ego Agenda, Don't Let It Run the Show

Most Breakdowns in Cooperation Are Caused by What People Do to Each Other's Ideas, Not by a Mismatch of Goals or Personalities

I've talked so far about the positive impact you can have on people by what you do with their ideas. Time now to look at the other side, at the problems created in your dealings with others when either you or they *don't* do right by each others' ideas. The size and pervasiveness of these problems is another well kept secret about people dynamics. It's a secret people keep not so much from each other as from themselves.

There's a powerful link between our ideas and our egos. Because of this a lot of our behavior is idea-driven — a lot more than we realize or like to think.

By idea-driven I mean either moved by the desire to shine a good light on our ideas, or activated by what someone else does to them. The secret isn't that we have these desires and reactions, it's how big a role they play in our success or failure to put people on our team. Most people see only the tip of this iceberg. Which is why they feel more amused than alarmed when I tell them this story.

THE IDEA THAT WASN'T THERE

Jeff, Joan, and their boss Stan are talking about what they can do to speed up development of new products in their company. Jeff makes a suggestion. Joan says she doesn't think they should do that and talks about the problem she sees with Jeff's idea. Jeff scratches his head and says "Good point, I hadn't thought of that." The discussion shifts to the status of a new product that is currently in a test market.

So that's that, you think, episode over. Jeff saw the sense in what Joan said, he didn't argue the point, he didn't seem to feel any need to defend his idea. But you find that the story hasn't ended. Ten minutes later the three of them are talking about How to get more value out of test market data. Joan says "You know, maybe we should do what we did at Acme. What we did ..."

She doesn't get to finish her sentence because Jeff interrupts with an objection. He says that Acme, where Joan used to work, is in a business that's very different from the one they're in. And that the kind of market testing that works for one kind of product and target customer seldom works when both are different. He tells a story to illustrate his point. Joan doesn't have a chance to say anything more about her idea because there are only a few minutes left before Stan has to go to another meeting, and he has two other issues he wants to discuss briefly before he leaves.

You find out later that Jeff didn't have a clue about what was done at Acme, and he interrupted Joan before she could tell him. His comment — that what works in one situation may not work in another — had some validity as a generality, but it may or may not have been true of the specific idea Joan had in mind. And that's where the idea still was, in her head and not out on the table. If there was no idea there for him to react to, what was Jeff's comment about?

That's easy, you say, it was a get-back reaction. Joan rejected his idea, so he rejected hers, sight unseen. Most people smile when I tell them the story, they don't act surprised. They've seen games like that being played in some of their meetings, out of the corner of their eyes if not center stage in their awareness. But they *are* surprised when I say that games triggered by what people do to each other's ideas are the major reason why meetings aren't productive. And that most breakdowns in teamwork and cooperation occur because someone gets careless with someone else's ideas, and not because of a mismatch in their goals or personalities.

That's the secret. And it raises three questions:

One, how can these things be?
Two, if they are true, why aren't we more aware of them?
And three, what can you do about it?

Let's take them one at a time.

You're Always Working at Least Two Agendas ... And So Is Everyone Else

To answer the first question you have to look into the nature of the link between our ideas and our self-esteem.

What makes it a powerful link

The need to think well of ourselves is one of the most powerful ones we have. Abraham Maslow, the motivation expert, placed it near the top of what he called our "hierarchy of needs." The need to boost or maintain self-esteem is behind a lot of the things we do (if you're in the advertising business you have a good working knowledge of this). Only a small segment of this behavior is relevant to this discussion — that which is idea-driven. It's a small segment but one that has a big impact on your dealings with people.

My idea-driven behavior gets activated in my dealings with you by the coming together of two things — the connection between what you say about me and my self-esteem, and the one between my self-esteem and my ideas.

Because we are social animals our self-esteem is based in large part on our perceptions of other people's reactions to us. This doesn't have to mean that you care a lot what other people think of you. You may care very little about that, but you still rely on others to confirm your idea of how good you are.

One consequence of being a social animal is that we depend on others to help us define what is real. Say you are in a roomful of people. You hear a noise. "What was that?" you ask. If everyone else in the room says, in effect, "What noise, we didn't hear anything," you begin to doubt whether you heard it yourself. Maybe you just imagined it.

As with the noise you thought you heard, so with your self-esteem. Other people's reactions to you are like mirrors in which you see yourself, and you use these glimpses to do a reality check on your self-image. This dependence on others is different from needing their approval. Not needing others' approval doesn't eliminate the "reality-check" dependence, but it does eliminate a lot of distortion from what you see reflected in their reactions to you.

Superimpose on this the other relationship — the one between self-esteem and ideas. We are not only social animals, we are also *thinking* animals. We identify with our minds. We think and therefore we are, or at least a part of us likes to think that. And we like to think that we think intelligently. Self-esteem has a lot to do with how smart we think we are.

John Holt, who spent a lot of time observing fifth-graders in their classes, noted that what the kids feared most was being thought stupid. This fear drove a large percentage of their responses to the questions posed to them by their teachers. Why, Holt asks himself, is being thought stupid so scary, and why is being called stupid "such a deadly insult to these children, almost the worst thing they can think of to say to each other?"

Ideas are ego extensions

Being called stupid doesn't stop being a deadly insult to people when they are grown ups. We know this so most of us don't go around at work calling people stupid, at least not to their faces. But we are not so careful with what we say about their ideas and opinions.

We identify with our minds and therefore with the products of our minds — our perceptions of a problem, our opinions about which of its causes is the most important, what we think could be done about the situation. These things are, in effect, ego extensions. Sticks and stones may not break my bones, but what you say about my ideas can really hurt me because it strikes at my self-esteem. If you say something that makes my ideas look bad you deliver a blow to my ego.

I feel the blow even if your intentions were pure — you may have said what you did not to make me look stupid, but because my idea raised a practical concern in your mind. But if I am not in charge of my idea-driven behavior I don't take this into account, I just react to the blow. Even if I care a lot about the task we're discussing my energy shifts into doing something about the blow — repairing the damage it caused or at least making sure I don't suffer any more of it.

Ways of counter-punching and keeping the chin covered

I can prevent further damage by not giving you any more ideas, or by giving you only those I think are the least open to attack — such as ones that are tried and true and therefore old and tired but safe to offer, or ones that I know you like.

"So here's this great bland idea"

I can try to repair the perceived damage done by your criticism of my idea by defending it, or by attacking one of yours. By blowing up one of your ideas I show you and myself that at least about that idea I am a more astute or thorough thinker than you. And proving that your thinking was flawed in this instance means, of course, that your earlier opinion of my idea was probably flawed too. One stone, two birds.

If you're my boss and you run rough shod over my ideas but I don't think it's prudent to do the same thing with yours I can hold my fire. I can wait until you ask me to implement one of your new ideas. Of course it won't work out as well as you hoped it would and you won't be able to pin it on me — I can say I did my best. Conclusion? Your idea wasn't great, you're not so smart yourself.

What you do to my ideas can also move me in the opposite direction. If you make them look good, I'm likely to be friendly to your ideas — I'll give them a good hearing, I'll be inclined to give them the benefit of the doubt, I'll be willing to help you move them forward. Again these reactions have little to do with your motives for doing what you did with my idea. You may not have been thinking at all about the effect of your response on me, you may have just liked the idea.

I react in all these ways because I'm not in charge of my reactions. And I'm not in charge primarily because I want to deny, for reasons we'll get into shortly, that I have such reactions.

The two agendas

What all this means is that whenever two or more people get together to talk about something, they are always working on at least two agendas. One has to do with the overt objective of the discussion — to generate ideas, to develop a consensus, to exchange information or perceptions about a situation, or to get some other piece of work done. I call this the *"task agenda."* (If it's a social occasion the "task" may be to comfort a friend, or to spend some time together pleasantly, or to keep yourself from getting bored.)

The second agenda has to do with the care and feeding of our "ego extensions." I call this the *"ego agenda."* Unlike the task agenda this one is worked on largely unconsciously. These two aren't always the only agendas present — people sometimes also bring with them political or other unstated hidden agendas — but there are always at least these two.

The costs

The ego agenda shows up in your dealings with people in several ways. It influences the choices you make about which of your ideas to present to others, and how to present them. It determines how open you are to their ideas. And it drives your reactions to what they do to your ideas. If you don't manage it, the ego agenda can make it very hard to do a good job of managing the people side of innovation.

The things people do to serve their ego agendas, both proactively and reactively, are the main reason why meetings aren't productive — as measured both by the amount of time it takes to get something discussed, and by the quality of the decisions that get made in them. In many discussions more than half the energy and creativity of the participants goes into playing games driven by their ego agendas, and not into getting on with the discussion's stated objectives. If you think of the number of discussions you have with people — formal or informal, face-to-face, or over the phone — the cost to you in time wasted alone is enormous, even if only a quarter of it is spent on these games.

And there are other costs. I've seen a lot of negotiations stall or fail altogether because of what someone on one side of the table said about an idea or opinion of someone from the other side. Maybe some breakdowns in teamwork and cooperation are unavoidable because of the presence of irreconcilable differences in goals or personalities. But the majority are the result of poor engagement process — they wouldn't occur if people didn't trash each other's ideas, however unwittingly.

Sometimes it isn't unwitting, people know they're doing it but think it's just a way of having a bit of fun with each other, no harm done. But there's always a lot more harm done than they think. Here's an example.

THE PLAN MAKERS WHO COULDN'T

I got a call from Sid, the head of the Information Technology group of a large company. He said he was having trouble getting his six section heads to agree on a two-year plan for the department. They had been squabbling about it for more than a month.

"I've got to have a plan to present to the executive committee in three weeks," he said, "and the way we are going we aren't going to have it unless I impose one on us." He didn't need a plan just to have a plan. This one was needed to show how they were going to deal with some tough business challenges. He was ready to impose a plan on his section heads but would prefer to not have to do it. He wanted me to run a planning session for him and the group to see if I could move them toward a consensus.

"But first," he said, "come sit in on our next meeting and tell me what you think the issues are that are keeping them apart. It isn't clear to me what the disagreement is about."

Sid also told me that in the past each section head produced a plan for his or her area, leaving it to him to put them together into a plan for the department. This was the first time he'd asked them to draft an integrated plan.

So I sat in on their next meeting, where I also couldn't identify any substantive issues that could be keeping the section heads from agreeing on a plan. Not that there weren't any issues for them to work on, but none of the ones I heard seemed like something that should be hard to resolve. And none of the section heads sounded like a troublemaker. But I did note that they were slapping each other's ideas around. It was all done in a jovial way, but their remarks had sharp edges on them. I didn't know what got them doing this, but I did know that once a group gets into this mode it can have trouble getting out of it. And as long as they are in it they are driven primarily by their ego agendas, and then minor task-related issues can become major hurdles.

I told Sid afterwards that I thought what was bogging the group down was their process because I hadn't spotted any major conflicts in their goals or interests.

"That's what I thought too," he said, "but I wasn't sure."

Later in the week they met again. This time I ran the meeting. For the first three hours I had to work hard to keep them from throwing darts at each other. I didn't have to do anything clever or complicated. If person B had a concern about something person A proposed, I got B to phrase it as a problem to be resolved by the group, instead of as a zinger aimed at A. I also did a lot of listening, something they hadn't been doing too much. Through me they started to hear each other's plan-related wishes and concerns. Just before lunch I sensed a change in the dynamics of the discussion. Instead of C and D manning roadblocks in the path E wanted to take, they began to help E get rid of them. This trend picked up speed after lunch.

At the three o'clock break Sid took me aside and said "I'm not asking you to do it, but you could go home now. I've got the consensus I need on the major pieces of the plan. All that's left is some details. Another hour and a half and we'll have those wrapped up too, now that they're all paddling together."

He was right, we were done with the details before five.

This isn't an isolated case. I could tell you a lot more stories with the same moral: if people get careless or cavalier with each other's "ego extensions," it's hard for them to work together productively.

Thwarting people's ego agendas makes two kinds of problems for you. The ones I've talked about so far are the more tangible ones — a meeting eats up a lot more time than it should, a negotiation stalls, a group has trouble agreeing about something. The other kind of problem is less tangible but just as real. It's the negative impact of trashing someone's intellectual property on the quality of your working relationship with that person.

This impact isn't easy to see because it isn't the result of any one thing you do or say. It is a reflection of the accumulated residue of the other person's reactions to all the things you do, over time. All you see is that a person you once could count on is no longer motivated to help you get things done. Or that someone's attitude toward you, once friendly or at worst neutral, has over time become adversarial.

Why We See Only the Tip of the Iceberg

Back now to the second of the three questions raised earlier. In essence, if the ego agenda drives so much of our behavior, how come we aren't more aware of it? There are several things that conspire to keep it hidden from the casual eye.

It goes against a fond self-image

We don't see a lot of our idea-driven behavior because we don't want to see it, for a variety of reasons.

Show someone like Jeff a videotape of his discussion with Joan and Stan. Stop the tape right after Joan rejects his idea and ask Jeff whether the rejection did anything to his blood pressure. I've asked hundreds of Jeffs (and Joans) a similar question in similar conditions. Eighty-five out of a hundred say they didn't feel a thing. When, a bit further on the tape, they see themselves doing things that are clearly a reaction to the rejection, most people seem genuinely surprised. The usual comment is "That's interesting. I guess I must have been bothered by it after all."

One reason why people deny, to others and to themselves, that they are bothered by what you do with their ideas is because the denial protects a fond self-image. We like to think that we are strong, mature, and reasonably task-oriented. If I'm like that then I ought not to be bothered by what you say about an idea of mine — hey, it's just an idea. O.K., being told it's no good may be a blow to my self-esteem, but it can't hurt me enough to divert me from the task at hand. Maybe someone who is overly sensitive or not quite grown-up, but not me.

Even in parts of the world in which people know that ideas are never "just ideas" and in which it is acceptable for adults to feel that they "lose face" when their ideas are knocked, *individual managers* still like to believe that though such knocks may bother them they don't allow this to affect their behavior. Videotapes of their discussions say otherwise.

Paradoxically, the more I deny that I feel the blow the more vulnerable I make myself to it, and the more blind to the ways in which I react to it. Telling myself that I'm immune to the blow doesn't stop me from reacting to it, it just drives my reaction underground where the decision about how to react is made by parts of me other than my conscious, reasoning self. And of course if I keep myself from seeing my reactions, I greatly underestimate the extent to which I cause them in others.

Denial takes some of the sting out of it

One woman, asked if she had been bothered by a colleague's trashing of one of her ideas, said "Oh no, you can't let something like that get to you. People do that to my ideas all the time at work. If I let things like that stick in me I'd be walking around looking like a pincushion. No, I don't mind that kind of give and take."

She too was surprised to see on tape what she gave back to her colleague a little later in the discussion.

I've heard others say similar things. It seems the denial does more than just protect a fond self-image. It also acts like a local anesthetic that dulls the pain of the sting.

We're not ready to see it

Something else that keeps people from seeing more than they see of the idea-driven behavior that is all around them is that very few of them know about growing ideas — how to do it and, more important, *why it makes sense to do it for task reasons*. Because they don't know these things they can ill afford to see more of the behavior — it would force them to think more about a problem for which they don't have a satisfactory solution. Best to let that dog sleep.

The problem is the one they face every time someone gives them an unacceptable idea. At some level they know that they — and therefore others — don't take kindly to being told that their ideas are no good. But they also think that the only responsible thing to do with such ideas is to get rid of them. The only question is how much time and trouble to take to soften the blow. What they actually do depends on the relative weights they give to their task versus their people concerns.

One way of trying to solve the problem

At one end are people who take great pride in being task oriented, and think that how others feel should always take a back seat to getting the job done. They think the thing to do with flawed ideas is to "tell it like it is" in the fewest words possible. They resolve any "task versus people" dilemma this may pose by minimizing it. They tell themselves that they can get away with their blunt way of responding to ideas because the people they are dealing with are grownups (and if they aren't that's *their* problem). And they can get away with it because the other person will see that their intentions are pure — they aren't trying to hurt anyone's feelings, they are just thinking about what's best for the task at hand. But telling themselves that they don't have a problem doesn't, of course, make it go away.

The other approach

At the other end are managers who think that you can't expect to get the job done right if you ignore people's feelings. These managers are willing to make an effort to take the edge off the rejection.

Taking the trouble to find a tactful way to say "Thanks, but no thanks" does indeed soften the blow — the other person senses that you are trying to be gentle. What it doesn't do is help that person to let go of the idea — to quit trying to sell it to you, to not bring it up again later in the discussion. And because the gentleness rarely makes people feel fully compensated for the rejection it doesn't keep them from becoming unfriendly to your ideas.

I also see managers take approaches that seem more expedient than caring. A common one is to say something nice about an idea before you shoot it. This may make you feel better but it seldom does much for the other person.

You can also pretend to misunderstand the idea. You can say "So what you're suggesting is ..." and then go on to talk about a different idea, one that you can buy. A variation on this is to say "Let me build on that ..." and then introduce an unrelated idea that is acceptable to you. In both cases you hope that the other person will either not bother to correct you, or be happy to take credit for an idea you seem to like. You may indeed succeed in getting rid of the original idea this way, but you seldom fool people about what really happened. Odds are they will feel manipulated and the consequences of that are usually worse than the reaction you're trying to avoid.

I've also seen managers use what I think of as the "make fog" approach. Give them an idea they don't like and they'll respond by throwing back a lot of words at you that don't exactly say no and don't exactly say yes or much of anything else. You're not sure what they are saying about your idea, or even whether that's what they are talking about. With such managers it's hard to know whether or not your idea is going to become part of what they decide to do, and you usually don't find out until after the decision has been made. And in most cases you find they've decided to do what they wanted to do anyway before they asked for your ideas.

In all cases, the problem remains ... so it's minimized

All these approaches leave something to be desired, and the people who use them know this deep down. And so they are not very open to the news that what they do with people's ideas is costing them more than they think. Not until they see that getting rid of flawed ideas, however gently or bluntly, doesn't make any sense *from a task point of view.*

If good ideas are the end-product of a process of evolution that usually starts with "bad" ideas, then there's a solid task reason for growing rather than killing them, whether with kindness or with a sharp knife. The reason for giving them a thoughtful look is to make sure you don't lose the seeds of the good ideas they contain, not to make people feel good — though that may be the happy by-product of the effort. But until people see this you can't blame them for wanting to minimize the impact of what they do with others' ideas. And in this the others collude with them, without meaning to, through their own need to deny the impact.

These needs to minimize and deny the existence of our idea-driven behavior is handsomely served by our ability to disguise it.

We are very good at making it look like something else

You can be looking for people's reactions to your comments about their ideas and not see most of them. Even something as straightforward as the earlier example of Jeff's "get-back" response to Joan can be missed because on the surface it looks like Jeff simply has a practical concern about her idea (will what worked at Acme work for us?). You can see what was really driving his comment when the episode is played back to you in slow motion, as it were. But in the heat of battle it's easy to miss what really happened. And people can get a lot more creative than Jeff was at dressing their idea-driven behavior in task agenda clothes. Here's an example.

THE OCCASION

I am working with a team of eight managers from the marketing division of a large food company. They are responsible for developing and putting in place a plan for introducing a new line of heat-and-serve meals into a very competitive market. They are with me for a couple of days to do two things: get some work done on their plan, and get some coaching on the process they use to generate ideas and make decisions.

What we'll be doing is to alternate between two activities — they discuss issues related to their plan, and then we review videotapes of the discussions. In these reviews we'll talk about what they did well and where there's room for improvement. I'll suggest ways for them to make these improvements and they'll try out these guidelines in their next discussion.

They're ready to jump into their first discussion. I suggest that before they do this they take a few minutes to talk about whether or not they are going to follow any procedure to discuss issues and develop ideas for them. Winging it is O.K., I say, as long as they're all clear that's what they're doing.

"Good idea," says Dave, and goes to the flip-chart. I go sit behind the video camera tucked away in the corner of the room.

They decide they should follow a procedure and quickly settle on one. Dave writes it on the flip-chart. The outline he notes isn't very different from the one most groups develop:

1. Define the problem (no solutions until we agree on definition)

2. Brainstorming (no negativity during listing of the ideas)

3. Select the best ideas.

4. Outline an action plan.

SUE ASKS A QUESTION

They start their discussion. Like most groups they soon stop paying attention to the procedure they've outlined and wander away from it.

About ten minutes into the discussion Sue has an idea for dealing with the issue they are talking about. Mike says "Oh Sue, we don't want to do that." He tells her why not. He can be funny, and the way he takes her idea apart makes everyone laugh. Sue laughs too.

Up to that point Sue has been one of the more talkative people in the group. But right after the exchange with Mike she goes quiet. She looks like she's still in the discussion, she leans forward to listen to people, she makes notes on her pad. But she doesn't say anything. I zoom the camera in on her every thirty seconds or so. Two minutes go by, not a word from Sue. Nothing until six minutes later, when Mike has an idea.

There are four people sitting on Sue's right, including Dave and Elizabeth. Mike and two others are on her left. Mike doesn't express his idea very well and I'm not sure the others have understood it. Before anyone can ask him to say more about it Sue turns to the people on her right and asks what seems like an innocent question.

"Are we following our procedure?" she asks, and looks at the flip-chart on which Dave wrote it. She looks at Elizabeth.

"I thought," she says, and lets her voice trail off.

"Gosh you're right," Elizabeth says, "we aren't following it. We aren't done defining the problem." She tells Mike he is out of order, it isn't time for ideas.

Mike starts to say something but Dave interrupts him. "You know what I think the real problem is," he says, and talks about how he sees it.

A couple of the others disagree with Dave and they get into a long discussion about the definition. Mike's idea is ignored. He tries to introduce it again but this time it's Dave who tells him it's premature to talk about solutions. Elizabeth tosses in her opinion about what the problem is, as does another person who hasn't said much until this point.

Mike gets up and goes to the flip-chart. He flips over the page with the procedure on it. He labels the next page "Solutions" and writes his idea on it. The group doesn't pay any attention to what he has written, they're busy with their debate about how to define the problem. Mike goes back to his chair.

A few minutes later Elizabeth gets up and goes to the flip-chart. "We ought to make a list of these definitions so we can vote on them," she says. She turns over the page with Mike's idea on it, and at the top of the next page she writes the word "Definitions." Under that she writes her definition and a couple of others. She sits down.

(Sue has got the group to ignore Mike's idea.
Watch Mike counter-react.)

Mike looks at his watch and announces that there are only fifteen minutes left of the forty-five scheduled for this discussion. "If we don't move on to listing ideas," he says, "we aren't going to have much to show for this session."

Dave says what good are ideas if they address the wrong problem. "Besides," he says, "if it gets us to a definition we can agree on I think it will have been time well spent."

Someone else says hey, if you define the problem correctly the solution becomes obvious. The discussion continues. Mike crosses his arms and starts to tap his foot. He frequently looks at his watch. He doesn't offer any opinions about what the problem is until the group is ready to vote on the definitions they've listed.

"All of the ones you have up there are O.K.," he says, "But they look at the problem from the wrong end. They look at it from our point of view, not that of the customer. He gets up and adds his definition to the list.

"That's what the customer would say the problem is," he says, and goes back to his chair.

Elizabeth and a couple of others tell him that their definitions do too take into account the customer's situation and needs, maybe he hasn't read the latest market research reports. They start to argue about what the reports really said. Time runs out before the group can get to a vote.

THE VIDEOTAPE REVIEW

After a brief break we watch the tape of the discussion. We stop frequently to talk about their process. When we get to the place where Sue gives her idea and Mike chops it up I stop the tape.

"Any reaction, Sue," I ask, "to what happened to your idea?"

"Nah," she says, "it was just an idea, and not a very good one as Mike pointed out. We don't take things like that personally on this team, we're very open and honest with each other."

I say O.K., and let it go for the time being. We watch more tape. After the camera zooms in on her a few times Sue starts to look thoughtful. I guess she has noticed that she isn't talking. Right after Mike gives his idea I stop the tape.

"Does anyone remember what happened next?" I ask. I don't look at anyone in particular.

There's a brief silence and then Sue sits up straight and puts a hand to her mouth.

"Oh my gosh," she says, "did I really do what I think I did?" She laughs. "But I was really creative about it, wasn't I?"

"You sure were," I say.

She turns to Mike. "Watch how I take care of you, big guy," she says.

Mike looks at her and then at me. He leans forward. I hit the play button.

When we get to the place where Elizabeth flips over the page with Mike's idea on it, everyone breaks up. When they stop laughing I restart the tape. By the time we're done watching it they all look thoughtful. They've seen how easily they can derail their discussions.

■ ■ ■ ■ ■

The ego agenda is worked on largely unconsciously. Once in a while, during a tape review, someone will say "Yeah, I realized right after I made that comment that I was reacting to what was said about my idea earlier." But this is rare. I continue to be impressed by our ability to fool ourselves into thinking we're doing A when we are really doing B, and by the creative ways in which we disguise the one to look like the other. But I am no longer surprised by these things.

What You Can Do About It

There are two parts to managing the ego agenda — what you can do about other people's idea-driven behavior, and what you can do to take charge of your own.

With others: Change how you act, don't try to change how they react

You can keep other people's ego agendas from getting in your way if you remember two things:

- You pay a big price if you get careless with people's ideas. It's easy to trigger hard feelings and defensive reactions, even when your intent is not to trash their intellectual property.

- There's a good *task* reason to look for the value in ideas you don't like, whether because they're flawed or because they just don't appeal to you.

Cultivate the "No, but ..." response

If you think of the ideas people give you as raw material and not finished product to which you have to say either yes or no, then you are free to say neither of these two things. Instead, you can say, in effect:

"The idea isn't acceptable as it stands. But let me tell you what I think it has going for it ..."

This means you're saying "No, but ..." instead of "Yes, but ..." You can talk about the idea's plusses, including some non-obvious ones, and then go on to talk about the reason(s) why the idea needs more work. If the plusses you mention are for real you disarm the other person — no need for that person to defend the idea or waste a lot of time trying to sell it to you.

You don't have to go on to tailoring or transforming the idea right then if time is short, or if you don't need to walk away with a workable new idea. This can be done later by you or by the other person. Or, given the pros and cons of the idea that you've helped the other person to see, that person may decide to let go of it and move on to another idea.

The only time you may have to say just "No" is when you must decide, right then, whether or not you are going to act on the idea as it stands, with no time to elaborate on the reasons for your decision.

What to do if you're offered more ideas than you can respond to in a thoughtful way in the time available? It's the best in such cases to respond only to the few for which you can do this — *and make no comment at all about the rest.* Make it clear that you consider these raw material, and that not saying no doesn't mean you're saying yes. No comment means just that, it's neither a tacit yes nor a less than straightforward no.

Convince yourself it's worth the effort

Responding to ideas as outlined above is not something that's hard to do, but it does take a bit more work than it does to look no further than an idea's obvious faults and dismiss it. And it takes some work to form any new habit.

There's a very clear incentive for doing the work when you are actively looking for a "better idea," or when you want to gain someone's commitment to a course of action. But it's easy to lose sight of the incentive for doing the work *as a general rule,* whenever you are presented with a flawed idea. In the absence of a compelling task reason, you will be doing it primarily to avoid costs that are not easy to see and therefore easy to minimize.

There's an easy way to convince yourself that it's worth doing the extra work. Do some experiments. Pick two comparable situations. In one do the work it takes to consistently give the "No, but ..." response to unacceptable ideas. In the other, just as consistently *don't* take the trouble to respond that way, perhaps even be extra "blunt." Compare the productivity of your interactions in the two situations. Compare also the amount of friction in your discussions and the stance the other person takes toward you and your ideas.

You can also do a "before" and "after" comparison. Pick a situation in which there's more heat than light in your discussions with someone. Start responding more thoughtfully to that person's ideas. Do it consistently for a while. Note changes in the nature of your discussions.

■ ■ ■ ■ ■

Two other things to keep in mind

- *Now that you know what to look for it won't be hard for you to see people doing things driven by their ego agendas. You won't see all the things they do, but you'll see more than you used to. You may find it tempting to tell people about the games you see them playing, in the hope that if you make them aware of what they're doing they will stop doing it.*

  Resist the temptation. Without a videotape you'll have a very hard time convincing them that they did what you saw them doing. It can even be difficult to do this with a videotape if you don't know how to make it a mirror they want to look at. They might listen to what you say you see them doing if they think you are an expert on the subject, but if they don't see you that way all you're likely to get for your effort is an argument.

- *For the thoughtful, "No, but ..." response to work, the plusses you mention have to be for real — things you really think are strengths or potential benefits of doing "something like that." If you don't believe this, you'll just be playing a game and others will sense it. And then they'll feel manipulated rather than disarmed.*

"But," people often ask me, "what if I really hate the idea and can't see anything that's going for it?" If you feel this way on occasion it will almost always be because you are doing one or more of three things:

- *taking the idea too literally*
- *forgetting that you are not trying to talk yourself into liking it as it stands*
- *allowing your ego-agenda to get in the way.*

■ ■ ■ ■ ■

Dealing with your own ego agenda

It's hard to do much about someone else's idea-driven behavior if you're not in charge of your own. You can take charge of it by doing two things:

- *Stay balanced.* The first thing to do is to stay centered, to not get knocked off-balance by what other people do to your ideas.

- *Rethink your looking-good strategies.* What are the things you do of your own accord, unprovoked, to show people that you're savvy and smart, or to keep them from thinking you're slow? Nothing wrong with wanting to do these things, but some ways of doing them are win-win, others are win-lose.

Let's look first at how you can do the first thing.

Keeping your balance

Say you and I are talking about an issue we need to tackle in a coordinated way. I make a suggestion. You tell me why you think it's a dumb idea. If I don't watch myself I'll get hot under the collar and react. I may tell you that you failed to understand my idea, and waste our time repeating it. (You may have understood it, just not liked it.) Or I may try to convince you of the idea's merits. Or I may shut up and sulk. But in all cases I won't be trying to listen to you.

If I become aware that your comment has knocked me off-balance *before* I react, I can regain my balance first. And from that centered place I can see that you weren't calling *me* dumb, you just have a problem with my idea, and you don't know about growing ideas. And then I can focus on trying to understand what you see wrong with my idea, and on thinking of ways to make it more acceptable to you.

The key to staying in balance is to keep track of the temperature under your collar — or of your blood pressure, or your pulse rate, whatever image works best for you. But to do this you have to be open to the possibility that what someone does to your ideas can raise the temperature a lot more, and a lot more easily than you like to think. This may not be a problem for you — you may not have that kind of fond self-image. Or, what you've read here may have convinced you that it isn't just immature or ultra-sensitive or insufficiently task-oriented people who get knocked off-balance by what's done to their ideas. And so it's O.K. if the same thing happens to you.

But if there's a part of you that still says "Yeah, but not me, I don't let things like that bother me," then for you reading about it is not enough. You'll have to gather some first-hand evidence for yourself.

The easiest way to get the evidence you need is to look for examples of idea-driven behavior in people you look up to, or at least don't look down on — people you consider reasonably grown-up and together. Just watch, don't try to prove or disprove anything. You'll see most clearly in situations in which you are relaxed, in which you don't feel rushed or tense. You'll see only a fraction of their idea-driven behavior but you'll see enough to convince yourself that the only people who *can* control their reactions are the ones who know they have them. And that the ones who act the most tough-skinned are the ones most easily thrown.

69

When you start keeping track of the temperature under your collar you may at first notice it only after the fact — after you've already reacted, unproductively, to what made it rise. But after a while you'll become aware of it *before* you react. The urge to react will pass if you are clear that it's O.K. to have it, just not O.K. to let it take over. You'll stay in balance. And then you'll discover how much power this gives you in your dealings with others.

You hit your best shots when you keep your balance

In tennis or golf or any other sport it's hard to hit a good shot if you are off-balance. The same thing is true of the "shots" you need to make in your interactions with others. But if you stay centered you can hit some great ones, even when you're playing with people more powerful than you.

Here's an illustration.

THE BOSS WHO LIKED TO BEAT UP IDEAS

John was a sales manager for a small but fast-growing company. I ran into him in an airline lounge a couple of months after he had been in one of my workshops. I remembered him telling me at the workshop that what he and his boss did with ideas was not so much to discuss them as have slugging matches about them.

"How's it going with the boss?" I asked him.

John grinned. "I was going to tell you about that," he said, "even if you hadn't asked."

His boss, he reminded me, was fond of coming on like a tough cowboy. He wore custom made boots to work. He believed that the way you got to a good idea was to put some on the table and stomp on them. If they survived that treatment they were O.K. If they didn't it was because they were weak ideas so it was no loss.

"In all fairness to my boss," John said, "he expects me to do the same thing to his ideas as he does to mine. The only problem I always had with this was that his opinions carry more weight than mine, so it was like being a welterweight in a boxing ring with a heavyweight. He and his ideas won most of the fights."

John said he got tired of losing so he decided to try a different tack.

"I was curious to see what would happen if I did two things: work at keeping my feet under me, and grow one of his ideas instead of trying to kill it."

A few days after he thought of it John got a chance to test this approach. His boss called him into his office to talk about something.

THE DISCUSSION

When John walked into his boss' office, there he was with his boots up on his desk.

"John, come in and sit down," he said, pointing to a chair on the other side of the desk. "You know that problem account we were talking about the other day? I know what you ought to do about it."

"And," John said to me, "he laid an idea on me that I didn't like at all. I wanted to take it apart. He had ripped into two of my thoughts on the subject the last time we talked about it, and I was still smarting from that. But I thought no, don't do the same thing to his idea, that's the game you always play with him and he usually wins. Tell him what you *like* about the stupid idea."

John said he also felt that he couldn't talk about the idea's plusses right away.

"That would have been too different from our usual way of going at things. If he thought I was trying something on him that I'd learned in some workshop he wouldn't listen to me. He'd tell me to quit fooling around and get back to straight talk."

So John started by saying the kind of thing his boss would expect him to say about an idea he disliked.

"Oh boss," John said, "you've got to be kidding. That's the worst idea I've heard all week."

When he said this John could see his boss squaring off for a fight. But before the boss could say anything John scratched his head and said "But you know, on second thought I can see some merit in it."

John mentioned one plus of the idea, and then a second.

"I thought I was just playing a game," John said, "but then I saw a couple of advantages of the stupid idea that I hadn't expected to see. I surprised myself and I know the tone of my voice changed when I talked about these."

John noticed that as he talked about these additional plusses of the idea his boss took his boots off his desk and leaned forward in his chair.

"He was listening to me," John said.

When he was done with the plusses John said, "But boss, I also have a serious problem with this approach of yours." And told him what this was.

And then, John said, something happened that had not happened before in any of their discussions. His boss got up out of his chair, came around to John's side of the desk, put his hand on John's shoulder and said:

"We can fix that little problem, we can fix that."

And the boss changed his idea to make it acceptable to John.

"For the first time in our relationship," John said, "it was 'we,' on the same side of the table, building an idea together. I walked out of there with an idea I liked, one tailored to *my* pros and cons, and my boss did most of that work."

THE AFTERMATH

John said that not all of his discussions with his boss since that one had gone as smoothly, but overall they were a lot more productive than they used to be.

"I still slip into our old pattern at times, but I know what to do if that gets us bogged down. Neither of us likes to give up on his

ideas, and we tend to dig in and stubbornly defend them when they're attacked. Our positions become entrenched and we become unwilling to grant that the other person might have a point."

If the argument is about one of his boss' ideas, John said he can get them out of it by saying, in effect: "O.K., maybe there's more to your idea than I can see right now. Give me some time to think about it."

"And if it's about one of my ideas, I can get us out of our dug-in positions if I remember that I can grow my own idea. Which means I can stop trying to defend every inch of it and start trying to understand what bugs my boss about it."

"Both tactics work," John said, "because I really do look hard at what's going for his ideas in the one case and, in the other, look for ways to fix what he thinks is wrong with mine."

■ ■ ■ ■ ■

Rethinking your looking-good strategies

Keeping your balance is about taking charge of your reactions to what others do to your "ego-extensions." To be fully in charge of your idea-driven behavior you also have to make conscious decisions about your looking-good strategies — the things you do, proactively, to show people how smart you are or to keep them from thinking you're slow.

■ Don't Let the Teenager You Once Were Make Today's Decisions for You

Our strategies for looking good — or for not looking bad — are developed early. Most are in place before we are done being teenagers. Most are based on what we see others do, and are acquired before we have the knowledge needed to do a good assessment of their pros and cons.

The strategies are too important to leave in the hands of the thirteen year olds we once were. They determine what kinds of thoughts we are willing to present to others, and how we express them. They influence the stance we take towards other people's ideas. They are our answers to some key questions: Does looking smart mean having only buttoned-up ideas? Does it mean being good at shooting down those of others? As a boss, does it mean you always have to have all the answers? Is it O.K. to say "I don't know" or "I like your idea better than mine"?

How you answer these questions depends on whether you are thirteen and want to impress your peers, or thirty-three and want to be good at making innovation happen. Over time our needs change, our capabilities grow, but many of our looking-good strategies stay the same.

There is, of course, nothing wrong with wanting to look good. Done right it's good for your self-esteem and it doesn't do any harm to your career. The question is how to do it in a way that doesn't have undesirable side-effects. You can, for example, try to look good to a roomful of people by being the best at having the last word, or being the best at understanding other people's words. One way may give you more instant gratification, the other better odds of finding good ideas and getting people behind them.

A transistor is a device that enables you to induce big changes at place Y by making small changes at place Z. A minor adjustment in the way you grip a baseball bat or golf club has a major impact on the flight of the ball. *And small changes in your looking-good strategies have a big impact on your ability to put people on your team.*

■ Taking charge

You take charge of your looking-good strategies by making conscious decisions about which ones you want to keep and which you want to modify or replace. Of course you first have to become aware of what they are, but this is not hard to do if you stop to think about them. Several may have come to mind as you were reading this chapter. If not, replay in your mind the last few meetings you were in — what did you do to look and sound smart, or at least smarter than someone else? It may take a while to get to know your more subtle strategies, but you'll quickly spot a few you'd like to tinker with.

How do you know whether there's much to be gained from changing any given strategy? What you've read here so far will give you a good feel for this in most cases. If there's any doubt you can resolve it by asking yourself three questions about the strategy:

- *Is it based on making me look good by making someone else look less good?*

- *Does it involve my taking more than my fair share of something, such as the available air time or the credit for an idea?*

- *Does it keep me from getting the most out of other people's ideas?*

If the answer to one or more of these questions is yes, then it's a strategy you can't afford to keep, not if you want your engagement process to be one that motivates people to help you make innovation happen.

■ Chuck the bathwater, not the baby

Discarding a strategy doesn't mean throwing away the things that make you good at using it. You may, for example, decide you want to quit trying to show how wise or clever you are by being quick to point out the fatal flaws in other people's thinking. But if what enables you to spot these flaws is a good eye for details or a good grasp of the practical realities, you don't want to stop using those assets. You just want to redeploy them in a more win-win way. What makes you good at spotting flaws also makes you good at spotting ways to fix them.

■ The core of an effective strategy

The most effective looking-good strategies I've seen are ones in which people employ, consciously or unconsciously, the following principle:

Compete against yourself, not others.

75

In the context of engaging people's minds this means that:

- You focus on doing as good a job as you can of extracting useful ideas and insights from other people's thinking, and you do this to meet the needs of the task at hand, not to "be nice."

- You *don't* worry about whether you're being smarter or funnier or nicer or more knowledgeable than the people you're with.

If you do these things, you engineer a triple win. The task wins. The process you use to make that happen makes other people look good and feel good about themselves. As a result *you* look good to them, without having to sell yourself or your ideas.

MANAGING THE EGO AGENDA: THE PRACTICE

What's in this section:

- *A Quick Review Summary.* If you want to revisit this chapter from time to time you can use this review to quickly remind yourself of the main points in it. If necessary, you can then read more about any of them in the relevant portions of the chapter.

- *A note about what your increased awareness may do.* You'll gain a lot from seeing more than just the tip of the iceberg of our idea-driven behavior. But for a short while you may become overly aware of it. This note describes what can happen and why it's not a matter of concern.

MANAGING THE EGO AGENDA: QUICK REVIEW SUMMARY

It's the Cause of Most Breakdowns in Cooperation

The ego agenda has to do with the care and feeding of our "ego-extensions" — our perceptions of a situation, our ideas about how to deal with it. It is driven by one of our most powerful needs, that which moves us to maintain or enhance self-esteem.

A major source of self-esteem is feeling intelligent. Because our ego-extensions are representatives of our intelligence, what's done to them has a direct impact on our self-esteem.

The ego agenda moves us to do things both reactively and proactively. The former are manifested in the way we respond to what others do to our ideas, the latter in our looking-good strategies.

The things people do to serve their ego agendas have a big impact on their dealings with others. The impact is much bigger than most of them realize. The costs include unproductive meetings, failed negotiations, and loss of motivation to help each other get things done. If you don't take charge of it, the ego agenda can make it very hard for you to make innovation happen.

Why We See Only the Tip of the Iceberg

The main barrier to managing the ego agenda is the tendency to minimize its impact on your dealings with others. It's easy to do this because several things conspire to make our idea-driven behavior hard to see:

- *We don't like to think that we can be knocked off-balance by what others do to our ideas. So we drive our reactions underground.*

- *Telling ourselves that we aren't bothered by criticism or rejection of our ideas helps to dull the sting of that treatment.*

- *If you don't have a good way of dealing with unacceptable ideas, you aren't open to the news that what you do now is costing you a lot more than you think. Best to let that dog sleep.*

- *We are very good at making the things we do to serve our ego agenda look like something else.*

What You Can Do About It

There are two parts to managing the ego agenda: what you can do about other people's idea-driven behavior, and what you can do to take charge of your own.

With others: Change how you act, don't try to change how they react

It's easy to trigger hard feelings and defensive reactions even when it is not your intent to trash people's intellectual property. There's something simple you can do to eliminate a lot of these reactions. There's also something you may be tempted to try that won't do this.

Cultivate the "No, but..." response

The best way to deal with unacceptable ideas is to think of them as raw material and not finished product. This frees you to say neither "yes" nor "no" to them. And to make it clear that an idea is *not* acceptable in a way that doesn't make the other person feel defensive ("Not as it stands, but let me tell you what it does have going for it ...").

Resist the temptation to tell them what you see

It can be tempting to tell people about the ego agenda games you see them playing. The hope is that if you make them aware of what they do, they'll stop doing it. But unless you're seen as an expert on the subject you'll find that in most cases you're pointing at a mirror that they don't want to look at.

Dealing with your own ego agenda

You can take charge of it if you do two things:

- *Stay balanced* — don't be thrown by the things people do to your ego-extensions.

- *Rethink your looking-good strategies.*

Keeping your balance

The key is to accept that you can be knocked off-balance a lot more easily than you like to think. Once you do that it isn't hard to keep an eye on the "temperature under your collar." At first you may notice it only after the fact — after you've reacted, unproductively, to what made it rise. But soon you'll start noticing it *before* you react, and then you'll act only after you've regained your balance. And find that this gives you a lot of power in your dealings with others.

Rethinking your looking-good strategies

You're not fully in charge of your ego agenda until you "own" the things you do, proactively, to show people you're smart or to keep them from thinking you're slow.

To "own" these strategies you have to be aware of what they are and to make conscious decisions about which ones you want to keep, and which you want to modify or replace. When in doubt, ask yourself:

- *Is it based on making me look good by making someone else look less good?*

- *Does it involve my taking more than my fair share of something, such as the available air time or the credit for an idea?*

- *Does it keep me from getting the most out of other people's ideas?*

If the answer to one or more of these questions is "yes" it's a strategy you can't afford to keep.

■ The core of an effective strategy

The most effective looking-good strategies employ the following principle:

Compete against yourself, not others.

In the context of engaging people's minds this means that:

- You focus on doing the best job you can of extracting useful ideas and insights from other's thinking — for task reasons, not to "be nice."

- You *don't* worry about whether you're being smarter or funnier or nicer or more knowledgeable than the people you're with.

A NOTE ABOUT WHAT YOUR INCREASED AWARENESS MAY DO

You May Go Through a Hesitant Phase — But It Will Pass

When I changed my blunt way of responding to people's ideas I gained something right away — there was less friction than there used to be in my dealings with them, and they were more willing to help me get things done. But I also lost something for a while.

There was less fluency and zip in my conversations. Before responding to people's ideas I thought more about what to say than I used to. Most people, including friends, didn't seem to notice anything. Except for two I was very close to. Both told me that I had suddenly started acting hesitant. Where, they wanted to know, was the person they knew and liked? (The people who care most about you are sometimes the biggest obstacles to change, though they don't mean to be. They want the best for you, but when you try to change for the better they want to hold on to the old you.)

The hesitancy disappeared and the fluency came back after a few months. My new way of responding became as automatic as the old way had been, something I did without having to think about it. This temporary loss of quickness may not happen to you, but if it does remember that it will pass. Or, it may happen but not be something anyone else notices if you are more of a muller than a talker. Mullers like to think before they speak and don't mind pauses between what someone says to them and their response. But if you're a talker, always ready with words, then your brief period of hesitation — if it occurs — will be a more visible change in your style than it will be if you're a muller.

The Awareness May Get a Little Loud — This Also Will Pass

The second thing that happened to me in this transition period between the old and new habit was that I became overly conscious of people's idea-driven behavior. It was akin to what happened to me in college one semester when I went out on a lot of field trips with a friend who was very knowledgeable about birds.

After I did that, a walk through a stretch of woods with friends became a different experience than it used to be. Before, the sound of birds was like white noise in the background. Every now and then the voice of a crow or jay would register, but except for those few seconds my attention was focussed on my conversation with my friends. After my field trips there was a dimension to the sound of the birds that had not existed before, and it has stayed with me ever since. But for a while I also had trouble paying attention to what my friends were saying because I was listening to the birds.

If you find that you are paying a little too much attention to the ego agenda, you'll also find that your awareness of it will soon move off center stage and into the background where you will focus on it only when you want to.

It's Their Loss, Not Yours

There is one more thing to watch for. You will start to give more thoughtful responses to people's "not all there" ideas, you'll put in the effort it takes to look past their obvious flaws. But other people aren't going to return the favor. If one of your ideas has even the smallest weakness in it, you'll hear about that and not much else. If this starts to feel unfair remember that you are doing what you do for solidly selfish reasons — you don't want to pay the price of not doing it. It so happens that what you do is also good for other people's self-esteem, but you're doing it primarily for what's in it for you.

Remember also that they don't know what else to do with your ideas.

MANAGING THE EGO AGENDA:
AT-A-GLANCE SUMMARY OF THE HOW

With others: Change how you act, don't try to change how they react

- **Cultivate the "no, but ..." response**
  ("It's not acceptable as is, but let me tell you what I think it has going for it ...")

- **Resist the temptation to tell them what you see**
  (It's hard to get people to see the ego agenda games they play.)

Dealing with your own ego agenda

- **Keep your balance**
  - keep an eye on the "temperature under your collar"
  - remember you hit your best shots when you are balanced.
- **Rethink your looking-good strategies**
  - When in doubt, ask yourself if it:
    - is based on looking good by making others look less good?
    - involves taking more than your fair share of things like air-time or credit for ideas?
    - keeps you from getting the most out of others' ideas?

    (You can't afford to keep it if any of the answers is "yes.")
  - The core of an effective strategy:

    Compete against yourself, not others.

4

■ The Role of the First Two Rules – A Reminder

The first two rules are at the core of what you need to do to engage minds and hearts. You'll need to use the principles associated with them to get the full benefit from using the rules that follow. Here's a picture to keep in mind.

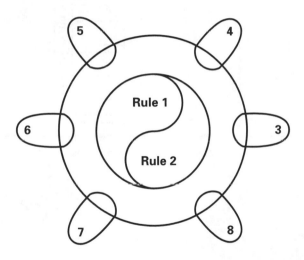

Keep in mind also that the increase in your effectiveness — at making innovation happen — won't occur in a linear fashion, in eight equal steps as you make each rule a part of the way you are with people. It's likely that more than half the increase will come with the use of just the first two rules. This is because using them gets you past the two biggest barriers to effectiveness. These are:

- not knowing how to extract good ideas out of the "raw material" people give you,

    and

- the ego agenda — if not managed.

Here again is the diagram that was used earlier to represent how the increase in your effectiveness is likely to occur.

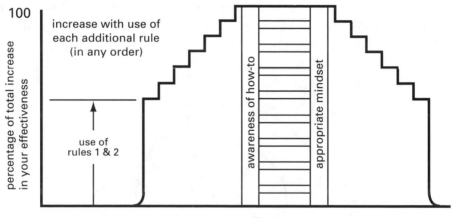

steps to greater effectiveness

5

■ Rule 3: Practice the Art of Hands-on Listening

Know When to Grab the Controls

If you want to get the most out of people's ideas you have to do a good job of listening both to and for them.

Listening is something we do most of the time without thinking about how we are doing it. We do it, so to speak, on automatic pilot. Everyone I talk to about it agrees that it's important to listen in a more hands-on way from time to time. But I seldom see anyone doing this. People don't do it because they aren't clear about both *when* to do it and about *what* to do in these circumstances. Or because they know these things but forget to grab the controls.

The situations in which it pays to switch from the auto to the manual mode are, of course, those in which you are most likely to either not hear something or misunderstand what you heard.

You know about two such situations. One is when what someone says triggers strong emotions in you. The other is when you bring to the discussion a lot of preconceptions about a problem or its solutions. You also know what to do in these situations (check your understanding often, even when you think you know what the other person means). So I won't say more about these situations here, other than that they are the ones in which it's also very difficult to remember to do what you know you should do.

But here are two other situations you may not know as much about, and in which it's both profitable to listen in a hands-on way and not hard to do it.

When It Sounds Like an Old Idea ... Listen for the Difference

Someone once said to me that it's not possible to have a new idea for a movie or a play. If Shakespeare didn't already think of it, one of the ancient Greek or Indian or Chinese writers did. This is, of course, both true and not true. It may not be possible to think of a basic theme that's not found in one of their works — man meets woman, man loses woman, man finds woman again, or the other way around. But it is possible to think of endless variations on the basic theme, and to add new details to them. If these new twists are good ones they transform the old themes into movies and plays that are fresh because they are made relevant to our time and situation in new ways.

The same thing is true of many of the ideas you get from others. The newness is usually to be found in the details and not in the basic concept. This is especially so for ideas about "people" problems. There are, for example, only a handful of basic approaches for motivating people to do something (make it rewarding, show them the stick, tailor the inducement to the person). That doesn't mean someone can't give you a fresh idea for how to make one of these approaches work for a given person in a given situation.

But it's not easy to hear the fresh part of ideas, whether these are for "people" or other kinds of problems.

The difficulty is created by the tendency to focus on the familiar — to hear the part of the idea that's similar to something you've already thought of or tried, and to then jump to the conclusion that the two are the same in all essential respects. Once you label an idea "known" there's not much reason to keep listening to it. And so you miss the potentially most useful part of the idea — that which is *different* from the "known." Here's an example of what you can do to keep this from happening.

THE SITUATION

Mel, the Director of Research for a pharmaceutical company, is meeting with his three section heads, Carl, Eleanor, and Ravi. This is the first of a series of discussions he intends to have with them and with some of their people. He wants to get their ideas for changing the way researchers interact with and are perceived by the other divisions.

The change is necessary, he explains, because they are not doing a good enough job of being accessible to and staying current with the needs of their primary customers — in their case the marketing and manufacturing divisions of the company. In recent discussions with the heads of those divisions he discovered that their budgets for the next year will include, in both cases, increases in spending on outside technical consultants. The increases are large enough to draw attention and raise questions about the value of the Research Division.

Both the other divisions have always spent some money on outside consultants, but in the past they have looked primarily to Research for answers to their technical questions. About two years ago they started to spend a lot more on this outside help. Why has this happened?

Not, Mel was told, because it was thought that people in the Research division weren't qualified to provide this help. Tony, the V.P. in charge of Marketing, put it this way:

"The impression my people have," he said, "is that your folks think their job is to focus on long-term "science" questions, and that they see getting involved in our more everyday concerns as an unwelcome interruption of that more important work."

He added that researchers were not very available, either to help solve problems or to take part in discussions in which his people reviewed the company's markets and products.

"Of course," he said, "this doesn't apply to all your people. Some are very willing to work with us. But there aren't many of them."

In a separate conversation Mel was told essentially the same thing by the head of the Manufacturing Division.

THE DISCUSSION

Mel reminds his section heads that providing consulting services to the other divisions is part of Research's mission statement. As is staying current on their needs.

"I know it's easy for researchers to lose sight of this part of our job," he says, "and I intend to do a better job of reminding them of it. I'll need you to back me up on that. But to effect a change in attitude we are going to have to do other things too, as part of an on-going campaign. Any thoughts about what some of those things could be?"

There's a brief silence. Then Eleanor, who has been with the company for about six months, says:

"I think part of the problem is that researchers don't have enough contact with people from the other divisions, not on any regular basis. If you don't feel connected to people you don't go out of your way to help them. Maybe we need a mechanism for getting our people to do more mixing and talking with the others. Could be a monthly briefing meeting at which people from all three groups talk about what's happening in their areas.

"We did briefings," Ravi says. "Didn't go over very well. We put a lot of work into them but got only a lukewarm response from people in all three divisions. So we gave up on the idea after a while."

"Oh," says Eleanor, "I didn't know that. I guess we'll have to think of something else."

"Before we do that," Mel says, "I want to make sure we're talking about the same thing. You weren't here when we ran those briefings, maybe you had something different in mind. Ravi ran that project, he can review what we did and you tell us if what you were thinking was different in any way."

Ravi says "Well, the idea was to have people from each group give brief presentations of their division's major accomplishments and challenges. The first few briefings were held every two months."

"So these were summaries of what was happening at the division level?" asks Eleanor.

"That's right," says Ravi.

"I wasn't thinking of anything that formal," says Eleanor, "and my idea was that people would talk about what was going on at the level of their jobs and projects. I thought maybe a monthly get-together of a few people from each division on a volunteer basis. They could meet over dinner, someplace where they could get a private room.

"Sure is different from what we did," Mel says. "I like the volunteer aspect. And it wouldn't require much preparation. What we did was to assign people to prepare and give the briefings. They had to put a lot of work into it to come up with a snapshot of the division that wouldn't upset any group in it. After the first two, no one wanted the assignment."

Carl says "I think that was also because people knew after the first couple that the briefings didn't stir much interest. There weren't any surprises in them, and you didn't learn anything about the issues faced by people at your job level in other divisions. That's the key difference here, why I think this idea will be better received."

"Sounds like something we should do," Mel says. He likes the idea that has emerged. He thinks some details need to be thought through — how big should the group be, how to get them to do a bit of work but keep it relaxed and informal, how to keep one or two people from grabbing all the air time. But these questions mean he has an opportunity to get Carl and Ravi to help develop Eleanor's idea.

Carl suggests the first few get-togethers be limited to no more than fifteen people, to give everyone a chance to do some talking.

Ravi says "Maybe we should give them a bit of structure. Like start with each person taking no more than a minute or two to describe one current challenge in his or her job, and maybe one success story related to it. After that they could break up into smaller groups or even pairs to talk more about some of those things."

"What that would do," Mel says, "is to make sure everyone gets to be on stage right at the start of the evening. Maybe it isn't important what they talk about after that, as long as they enjoy themselves and get to know each other. One objective of these get-togethers is for people to learn about each other's work. But the other is to develop personal links at their level. It's the second one that I think is more important."

Carl says "I'm sure there are a few people in each division who would like to do this, enough for the first couple of events. Maybe we should ask these groups to give us their ideas for what else we could do to develop those personal links."

"Nice add-on," Mel says. "Reminds them that's an important objective of these get-togethers. And allows them to help shape the larger campaign of which these events are a part. Anyone see any reason why we shouldn't go ahead with this idea?"

No one raises any objections.

"Okay," Mel says, "any other ideas?"

■ ■ ■ ■ ■

The problem with listening to any idea is that what the other person says is a kind of verbal short-hand for the thoughts and images in that person's head. The words trigger a set of thoughts and images in your mind.

Misunderstandings occur when the set in your head is different in some essential way from the set in the other's head, and neither of you does anything to find out if this is the case.

You are least likely to check the differences between the two sets of thoughts when the other person's idea sounds familiar. The words in this case bring to mind thoughts of what you did — or are doing, or are thinking of doing — that is similar. The tendency at this point is

to jump to the conclusion that the other person meant precisely that. And then, of course, you stop listening — no need to hear any more, you already know all about it, nothing new there.

How to listen for the difference

The most effective way to deal with the tendency to leap to the conclusion that you "know all about it" is not to fight it. Instead of trying to keep yourself from doing it, use its end-product as a cue to switch from auto to manual. Whenever you find yourself thinking or saying "I've already thought of that," or "We did that," make that a signal to grab the controls and *listen for the difference.*

You can check for differences between your idea and what the other person suggested in one of two ways. You can do what Mel did — say, in effect, "We'll tell you what we did, then you tell us if your idea was different in any way."

Or you can do it the other way around — first ask the other person to say more about his or her idea, and then describe yours and talk about the differences between the two.

Which way you go about it depends, first, on which you think will make the other person feel free to say more about the idea. If you think the other person will be happy to talk about it either way, then it depends on which way you think will be quicker at bringing out the differences.

What you'll get out of it

If you take the trouble to listen for the difference you'll find that more often than not you'll unearth a useful idea — either one that's different enough from yours to call new, or one that represents a twist on it that makes the old one more effective. But, as with the other rules in this book, when you use this one you get more than just a useful idea.

By doing some hands-on listening Mel was able to make a start at getting commitment, from his section heads, to help him with his campaign. He did this in two ways. One was by giving them a sense of having a piece of ownership in the "intellectual property" on which the campaign will be built. At this stage Eleanor may have more of this sense than Carl or Ravi because she provided the "different" idea. But because they helped to grow it they will also feel they own a piece of it.

But the commitment Mel began to build goes beyond that which comes from people feeling that they own a piece of a concept. When you listen to someone in a hands-on way you send that person a powerful message: I think your ideas are worth listening to with care.

A sense of ownership in a plan creates commitment that is directed primarily at that plan. But by proving to people, by the way you listen and respond to their ideas, that you value and respect their thinking you build commitment that is directed primarily at *you* — at helping you to accomplish something. And you build this kind of commitment *even when your attempt to involve them in the development of a plan doesn't produce any fresh ideas.*

The most productive involvement is, of course, one that builds commitment in both ways. A discussion that produces a "better" idea generates excitement, especially if the production requires some creative thinking. But if I could build commitment in only one way, I'd choose the second one. The commitment you build by making people feel valued and respected is quieter but deeper. It is also broader — it motivates people to help you with not just the innovation you're talking about now, but also ones you may talk to them about in the future.

■ ■ ■ ■ ■

94

A note about the practice

You may find it easy to train yourself to listen for the difference, to keep on rather than stop listening when you find yourself thinking or saying "done that, thought that." But if you find that it's harder than you thought it would be to make this response second nature, then you may need to grab another set of controls — those that run your ego agenda.

Dismissing other people's thoughts as "old hat" can be a way of telling yourself and others how much you know, how thoroughly you've already thought about or dealt with the situation. Your ego agenda can make you reluctant to admit that there's an important bit in the other person's idea that you hadn't thought of yourself.

Your ego agenda is most likely to get activated in this way in situations in which you *have* already given a lot of thought to something, or in which you are a subject matter expert. But this also makes them the ideal ones in which to start to train yourself to listen for the difference. If you establish the habit first under tough conditions, it takes very little effort to extend it to other, easier ones.

■ ■ ■ ■ ■

When You're Asked for Information ... Dig Out the Thought Behind the Question

When you ask people for their ideas they don't always give you all the ones you'd like to hear. If you want to hear them, you have to dig for them. How do you know when it's a good time to dig, and how do you do the digging?

A good time to dig is when people ask you for information about a situation for which you want their ideas. If you draw out the thinking behind these questions you'll find that their purpose is seldom what it appears to be — to elicit information that will fill a gap in the asker's understanding of the situation, period. This may be so in three cases out of ten, but in the other seven the question is either a *scout* for or a *camp follower* of an idea the asker has.

It's a scout when the other person isn't sure about the value of the idea. The purpose of the question is to gather information that can be used to judge whether the idea is good enough to be shown to you.

The question is a camp follower when the asker has already decided the idea is not good enough to put on the table, but it has directed the asker's attention to the issue the idea was designed to address, and asking for information feels like a safer way to talk about the issue than offering an idea you could easily shoot down.

People withhold these ideas from you because they either don't know or forget that it's O.K. to give you flawed or half-baked ideas, that you're good at squeezing something useful out of such raw material and won't make them look stupid for having given it to you. If you're the one who knows how to get the most out of an idea, you should be the judge of its value to you, not the other person.

Here's how to dig.

THE SITUATION

Kate is the Executive Director of a non-profit organization that provides services to needy children. Small- and medium-sized businesses are a good, steady source of contributions. Kate thinks it's important for her to meet with the owners of these companies at least once a year. She's found that many of them participate in trade shows, and that if she picks the right shows to go to she can schedule, over a couple of days, meetings with a half dozen or more sponsors. She also finds that her meetings with them are more relaxed in these settings than they are in their offices.

In her meetings with them Kate gives them a brief review of where their dollars are going, and of what's happening with the services her organization provides. She also asks them for their ideas about how she could provide those services more effectively. She's found it useful to get this business perspective on how to run things.

Kate is meeting over lunch with Ari, whose company has been a contributor for several years. Kate has finished her review. Ari has just ordered some coffee.

THE DISCUSSION

Ari takes a sip from his coffee and looks at Kate. "How do you find new corporate donors?" he asks.

"Mainly through mailings to people selected from a bunch of lists we buy," Kate says, "and through referrals from people like you."

Kate knows about questions, so she digs.

"What were you thinking?" she asks Ari.

"Nothing much," he says, "just an idle thought that came to mind."

"And what was that?" Kate asks.

"Not something you'd ever do. An image of you at a trade show like this one, only you and some other non-profits were putting it on. But I know what it costs to do these things, no way you all would want to spend that kind of money. And for what? You'd have a hard time getting any prospective donors to come to it. As I said, not a serious idea."

Kate also can't see a "trade-show" for non-profits but in her head Ari's idea gets transformed into something she *can* see happening.

"You just gave me an idea," she says. "What if I approached you, and several of our other contributors who are here, to sponsor a booth for me at this trade show next year? Our display would tell our story but it would also highlight all of you. You give to a good cause, why not let it be known?"

"Yeah, why not?" says Ari. "Not a bad idea. It would depend on your being able to get enough other companies to go in on it so the cost to each one would be manageable."

"I'll talk to the others and get back to you," Kate says. "Thanks for the idea."

"You're welcome," says Ari.

■ ■ ■ ■ ■

Note that Kate answered Ari's question before she dug to see if there was an idea there. You can irritate the other person if you don't provide the information sought and instead answer the question with another question that says, in effect, "Why do you want to know?" This, in Ari's case, could have provoked him to say or think "Just answer my question, none of your business why I asked it."

When she did dig, Kate did so by asking:

"What were you thinking?",

and not:

"Did you have an idea?"

There are two reasons why one works better than the other. One is that the first question conveys a minimum of expectations about what you hope to find by asking it. You're interested in whatever thoughts the other person had, they don't have to be "ideas" or even directly related to the subject at hand. What the other person considers a stray thought could, by association, make you think of something that is relevant. The lower the expectations you create with your question, the easier it is for the other person to answer it.

The second reason why it's better to dig with one kind of question than the other is that if you ask people whether they have "ideas" they may say "no," again for either of two reasons. One, they think that what they have in mind is *not* a good idea, and good ones are the only ones you want or the only ones they feel it's safe to talk about. If they did think it was any good — or felt O.K. talking about it even if it wasn't —you wouldn't have to dig for it. They'd have told you what it was either after asking you the question or without having to ask it.

The other reason people may say "no" is that they may not be aware that they have an idea. In my work when I dig out ideas people often come to me afterwards and say "I didn't know I had that idea until you dragged it out of me." It seems an idea doesn't have to be in the lit part of your mind's stage for it to prompt a question (of either the scout or the camp follower kind). It can do so from the stage's unlit wings. And the information the question elicits can be used, in the wings, to judge and label the idea unfit for the stage.

■ ■ ■ ■ ■

Practice note

Here again, as in listening for the difference, your ego agenda can make things difficult if you don't watch for it. It's nice to be asked for information about something you know more about than the other person. Makes you want to take the podium, tell 'em what you know. And in the process forget that the real opportunity here is to dig for an idea. The more you really are an expert compared to the other person — because you are more familiar with the specifics of the situation, or because you know more about the subject in general — the easier it is to forget to *answer the question you're asked briefly, and then get the other person talking.*

If you want to dig for ideas but find that you tend to forget to do it, you can create a simple reminder for yourself. You can scribble just the letter "Q" or "Dig Q" in a corner of a note-pad (or laptop screen) , if either is handy. If these things won't be around or you don't want to use them, you can stick a small self-adhesive dot — with or without anything scribbled on it — on something you're likely to look at often (your pen, or watch, or waterglass, whatever).

If you use the reminder on enough occasions you eventually won't need it — it will become ingrained. What's enough is different for different people, but it can be as little as just a couple of times.

DOING MORE HANDS-ON LISTENING: QUICK REVIEW SUMMARY

Know When to Grab the Controls

Listening is something we do, most of the time, on "auto pilot." There are two situations in which it's both profitable to listen in a more hands-on way, and not hard to do this. These are:

• When it sounds like an old idea

We tend to focus on the familiar — to hear the part of someone's idea that's similar to what we've thought of or tried. We tend to *not* hear the part that's different and therefore capable of adding a dimension to our thinking.

To listen for the difference in a hands-on way:

- When you find yourself thinking or saying "I've thought of that," or "we did that," make this your signal to grab the controls and check for the difference.

- You can check for the differences by either:
    - first explaining your ideas, and then asking others how theirs are different,
    - or first asking them to say more about their ideas, and then talking about how you think these are different from yours.

• When you're asked for information (about the situation for which you want ideas)

When you ask for ideas, people often don't give you all the ones they have. But they often give you a clue that this is the case — by asking you for information. Such questions are usually either a scout for or a camp follower of an idea.

It's a scout when the purpose of the question is to gather information that can be used to judge whether the idea is good enough to show you.

It's a camp follower when the asker has already decided the idea isn't good enough to show you, but the idea has directed the asker's attention to the aspect of the situation the idea was designed to address.

To dig out the thought behind the question:

- Provide the information sought ... *briefly.* (Avoid answering the question with the question "Why do you want to know?")
- Then get the other person to say more about what was on his or her mind.
  ("What were you thinking?", not "Do you have an idea?")

Notes About the Practice

The why and how of doing hands-on listening is straightforward. What can make it hard to do is the ego agenda.

• In listening for the difference

Your ego agenda can make you reluctant to admit there's an important bit in the other person's idea that you *hadn't* thought of yourself. And dismissing others' thoughts as "old hat" can be a way of telling them — and yourself — how well you've already thought about or dealt with a situation.

These things are most likely to happen when you really *have* given a lot of thought and attention to a situation.

• In digging out the thought behind the question

Being asked for information can make you want to "take the podium." If you do that, it's easy to forget that you have an opportunity to uncover an idea.

101

This is most likely to happen in situations in which you really do know more than the other person about the general subject, or about the specifics of the situation.

The key to taking charge of your ego agenda in these situations, as in all others, is to be aware of the things that activate it. And to be aware of the costs, in these situations, of letting it run the show.

What You Get from Doing Hands-on Listening

Both the "fresh air" and the "clean water" needed by the innovation process:

- Ideas you wouldn't have otherwise heard, from which you can extract ones that increase the effectiveness of your action plans.

- Increased motivation and commitment not just to help you implement specific ideas, but to help you do things in general — to be on your team.

DOING MORE HANDS-ON LISTENING: AT-A-GLANCE SUMMARY

When to switch from the auto to the manual mode	How to clarify or dig for the other's thought
When you're looking for ideas AND:	
You find yourself thinking or saying "It's the same as my idea — nothing new there"	Listen for the difference • either talk about your idea, then ask others in what ways theirs' may be different • or first ask others to say more about their idea, you listen for and talk about the differences
You are asked for information about the situation for which you want ideas	Dig for the thought beneath the question: • answer the question briefly, then draw out the other person "What were you thinking?"

6

■ Rule 4: Go Upstream ... If You Want People to Change Their Course

The Situation, the Usual Approaches, and the Better Alternative

In previous chapters I've described what you can do when someone gives you an idea you don't like, and it represents something *you* could do about a situation. But what do you do when you don't like the idea and it represents something the *other person* could do, and wants to do, and if done would cause you some grief?

If you have the power to stop the other person from going ahead with it, well and good. But what if you don't have this power, or feel that using it would damage your relationship?

Faced with this situation most people do one of two things. They either prepare to suffer silently if they think it would be unwise to try to talk the other person out of the idea — for example if the other person is a boss who will, they know, not take kindly to the attempt. Or, they *do* try to talk the person out of it by pointing out the idea's drawbacks or by presenting "better" ideas — or both. This works sometimes, but more often it hardens the other's determination to stick with the idea. The other person feels obliged to defend the idea from your attack and you become an obstacle in the path the other wants to take.

There's a third approach. It greatly increases the odds that the other person will let go of the idea. And it's an approach you can safely use with anyone, including that testy boss. In this approach the first thing, you do is to try to understand what's driving the idea, why the other person wants to do it.

The things people want to do are means for attaining certain ends. In the flow of their thinking the ends come first, and in that sense are "upstream" from the means. The more clearly you understand the ends the better you are able to think of other ways for people to attain them, ways that also don't cause you grief. And if you can't think of any such ways, your greater understanding of what's driving someone's idea will make it easier for you to live with it.

The example that follows illustrates how you can get someone to let go of an idea.

THE SITUATION

Linda, the head of the Market Research department of a company that makes household products, asks me to help her develop a reorganization plan for her group. She came into the job a year ago and thinks that her department is not as effective as it could be even though the people in it are reasonably competent. She wants me to do two things. One, help the planning team — Linda and her four section managers — to think innovatively, meaning not being constrained by their old ideas about how things should be done. The second thing is to provide a process for gaining buy-in for the plan the team develops from both her people and from key customers.

Market Research is a centralized corporate function. Its "customers" are the company's three marketing divisions,

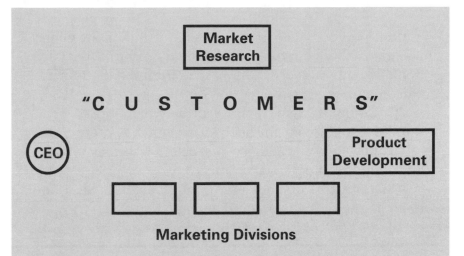

the product development division, and the CEO for whom they develop a monthly report on market trends.

Linda and her managers like the process I propose, except for one piece of it. And this is my suggestion that as part of the first step I interview several "customers," including the CEO and the heads of the four divisions.

"Why do you want to interview them," Linda asks, "why not get the information you want through a question-naire?"

I tell her I thought about questionnaires. They could be sent to a lot more people than I could interview in a rea-sonable amount of time. But I came out in favor of inter-views because it's a lot of work to develop a good ques-tionnaire, and because in a discussion people feel more free than they do on paper to say things other than those required by your questions. I would also get to know the customers from whom we most wanted to get buy-in for the plan.

"But," I add, "it sounds like you've got some other thoughts about this."

"It's the feel more free thing that bothers me," she says. "Yes you'll learn more if they don't limit themselves to answering your questions, but what if they start giving you ideas about how we should be organized? What if we don't like those ideas? If they come from the big folk, we can't just ignore them."

"Good point," I say, and describe what I would do to unhook people from any such ideas that they mentioned.

"Hope it works with these characters," she says. "O.K., I'll set up the interviews for you."

What follows happens in my interview with Jack, the head of one of the marketing divisions.

THE INTERVIEW

Jack quickly makes it clear to me that he isn't happy with Market Research. He has some good things to say about Linda and her staff — hard working, smart — but having got that out of the way he starts to talk about the ways in which he thinks the department is hampered by its own rules and procedures.

"Keeps them from thinking smart," he says, "about how they do their research and about what else they could be doing for us. You can't be creative and you can't be proactive if you attach too much importance to doing things by the book."

He thinks the department's way of working is a legacy of Linda's predecessor. He had hoped she would shake things up. But it's been almost a year since she took over and he can't see that much has changed. He tells me about a couple of business opportunities that his division didn't get its hands around "because Research didn't alert us to them quickly enough, so competition got there first." This happened six months ago but I can see that he's still upset about it.

I ask him to describe some of the qualities of what he would consider an ideal Market Research department. He gives me a thoughtful answer. I ask him a few other questions. We're done with the interview with a few minutes left of the time allotted to it. As I get ready to leave he says:

"And tell Linda that I'm going to propose at the next Management Committee meeting that I take five of her people and put them on my floor. Got an office I can put them in. Had the thought at the back of my mind for a while, time to do something about it."

Whoops, I think, this could be trouble. There are only about twenty-five people in Linda's department. If he takes five, the other three divisions may want to do the same thing, and that'll be the end of Market Research as a centralized function. I knew the CEO preferred it to be independent of the divisions, but I was sure if the heads of all three marketing divisions wanted to do it he wouldn't oppose the move. One of them was designated to be his replacement. The CEO's unhappiness aside, the move would disrupt things for several months. The Research people would be distracted by it and it would be hard for them to keep their minds on their work. So I say:

"Interesting idea. May I ask why you would want to do that?"

"I'll tell you why," he says, "I'd be able to make sure those people stay assigned to my business long enough to know its needs. Every time I turn around I see new faces on the team that works with us. I know they like to move people around, it's part of their career development system. But it wasn't designed with the customer in mind."

"Good point," I say as I note it. (He told me at the start of the interview that it was O.K. so I've been taking notes all along.) "Anything else?"

"They have this formal style," he says, "come here only for scheduled meetings, don't mix much with my people outside them. I think people work together better if they know more about each other than just their name, rank, and serial number."

"Be hard for them to not do some mixing if they were on the same floor," I say.

"That's right," he says.

"Anything else?" I ask.

He thinks for a moment and then leans forward in his chair.

"There is something else," he says. "They have this rule. No comment about what they hear from a group of consumers until after they've run all kinds of checks to make sure what they heard is sta-

109

tistically valid. Nothing wrong with that, but in the real world we sometimes have to make quick decisions, we can't wait until they're done playing with the numbers. I can get the information I want but it's like pulling teeth. Who do they think I am? Someone fresh out of school who's going to make a rash decision based on something that may be one atypical consumer's opinion?"

He takes a breath and expels it through his nose, short and sharp.

"You know what else it would do," he says, "it would make it clear to them that this division's business was their number one priority, so I'd get better than coach class service from them."

I don't ask him to elaborate. I've heard that his division used to be number one in rate of growth and profitability, but has slipped to number two and, if the trend continues, it could soon be number three. So, I think, he feels he's being treated like a second-class citizen, not someone to whom you give first-class service.

I thank him for taking the time to talk to me. Before I leave I say:

"May I ask you for a favor?"

"What's that?" he asks.

"You know," I say, "that Linda is planning to reorganize her department, and that I'm helping her with that. One of the first things we're doing is to talk to you, the customers, to make sure the changes we make are driven by your needs. Would you be willing to wait a bit longer, not move forward with your idea, until after we have a chance to show you our plan?"

He looks at me and at the note-pad on my lap.

"Okay," he says, "you've been sitting there listening to me for forty-five minutes, I'll wait to hear what you have to propose. But I won't wait too long."

He gives me six weeks. The Management Committee, of which he is a member, meets every month. The next meeting is in two weeks. Jack says he won't raise his idea at that meeting.

"But I will at the next one," he says, "unless you give me a good reason why I shouldn't."

"Fair enough," I say. "Thanks."

THE FOLLOW-UP

We have to put in some overtime to meet Jack's deadline. Though the plan isn't all done by then we have enough in five weeks to take to Jack. It doesn't, of course, include moving five people to his floor. We've found other ways to do for him everything he thought the move would do, and more.

We plan to change the system used to reassign Research people. We propose that the decision to move people in and out of his group be made jointly by him and Linda, or Linda and one of his managers. The same offer will be made to the other divisions.

"Would you also be interested," Linda asks, "in you and your managers doing part of the performance appraisal of anyone assigned to your division?"

"Sure would focus their minds on the needs of our business," says Jack.

We propose several activities that would help people to get to know each other, activities that would include not just people from his division and Research but also people from Product Development. Jack likes that idea.

"We have the same problem with them," he says, "only worse because they're located ten miles away."

Planned changes in the way Linda's group operates include a mechanism that will make it easy for him — or anyone he designates — to get quick, "pre-validation" headlines of the things Market Research hears from consumers.

"As you know," Linda says, "many of the 'focus' group discussions we have with consumers are held in rooms with a one-way mirror, so several of us can watch but not inhibit the consumers with our presence. We could arrange a video link so you can watch too, live, right here from your office. That way you don't even have to wait for us to prepare the headlines."

> "Good idea," Jack says, "only the monitor should be on your floor, not here."
>
> The plan also includes things that address other concerns Jack expressed to me in my talk with him. Here's what he says to Linda when we're done reviewing the plan with him.
>
> "I think," he says, "that given these things you're talking about doing, there's no need to relocate your people. I know that's going to make some of *my* people happy. They've been eyeing that office I've kept open, we need a small conference room and that would be a good space for it."

The Difference Between Going Upstream and Growing an Idea

The things we want to do are our means for attaining some ends. We start thinking about the means after the ends form in our minds. Either or both kinds of thoughts can form at the unconscious level. But at whatever level the thinking takes place, the ends precede the means in our "flow of thought," and can be said to exist "upstream" from them. You "go upstream" to try to understand why someone wants to do something.

What we did with Jack's idea was, in effect, to transform it. But we did it in a way that's very different from the idea growing process described earlier.

Given an idea you don't like, you grow it when it represents something *you* can do about a problem, and the problem is one that you've posed. In these circumstances you can say "Let me tell you what that has going for it, and also what's not right with it ... how could we keep the one and fix the other?" Your pros and cons provide a blueprint for changing the idea to make it acceptable to you.

But when the idea you don't like represents something *someone else* could do and wants to do, you have to take a different tack. You'd still like to see the idea changed to one that's easier for you to live with, but how do you get the other person to be open to the change, and how do you develop the blueprint for that change?

You know what you *don't* like about the idea, so you have one piece of the blueprint. But the blueprint is not only incomplete, the part you have is one that doesn't have much relevance for the other person. Remember, the other person likes the idea. To complete the blueprint you need to find out *why* the person likes it — to uncover what doing that thing will do for that person. The next question is how to get that information.

Creating the right dynamics

If you say to me, about something I want to do, "Tell me what the plusses are of doing that," or "Let's look at the pros and cons of what you want to do," you'll set off an alarm for me. I'll think you want me to re-evaluate my decision, and I'll suspect that you've got some minusses in mind that you are going to use to counter any plusses I mention. If I tell you what I think they are, I'll do it in the spirit of combat, ready to defend what I want to do against your attack. Putting me in this frame of mind is not the best way to make me feel open to other ideas. And if I'm a touchy boss, you also have other reasons for not saying things that may make me feel defensive.

If I had said anything to Jack that made him feel I was asking him to defend his idea, he could have told me to go jump in the nearest swamp. "This is something *I* want to do," he could have said, "who are you?"

You set up very different dynamics if what you say makes me think you are interested in my situation, and in the problems related to it that I think the idea will solve for me. Your wanting to know more about these problems doesn't make me feel defensive if I think you just want to understand them, not question their validity. If anything, I'm apt to be flattered by your interest. And if you really are interested in my problems, maybe you're also interested in helping me to solve them. So okay, I'll tell you more about them.

To get Jack to tell me more about what was driving his idea I said:

"Interesting idea, may I ask why you want to do that?"

The exact words you use aren't important as long as they and your tone and your body language all give the same message: I'm interested in your situation, if there's something I can do to help I'd be willing to do it.

It's hard to fake this message. Most people will sense it if all you're interested in is getting hold of information you can use to divorce them from their ideas. You are most likely to set up the right dynamics when you're open to the possibility that what you hear may make *you* change your mind — you may see that doing what they want to do is, after all, the right thing for them to do. And that the right thing for you to do is to learn to live with any grief that causes you.

■ ■ ■ ■ ■

What You Learn Can Also Be News to the Other Person

People often decide what they want to do about a situation without being completely clear about the problems they hope to solve by doing it. This is especially the case if it's a situation about which they are upset or irritated, and if it's also one they haven't talked about to anyone. Thoughts can exist in our heads in a fuzzy state. Having to put them into words brings them into sharper focus.

After Jack agreed to tell me why he wanted to put some of Linda's people on his floor, the first two reasons came to him readily. (He'd have more control over how long they stayed assigned to his division. And, they and his people would get to know each other better.)

But he had to stop and think before he put his finger on the last two. (He'd be able to deal with his frustration with their unwillingness to give him quick headlines of what consumers said to them. And he'd be doing something about his concern that they weren't giving his business priority service.) I had the feeling that it wasn't until he talked about them with me that he became aware of how much these things were bothering him.

The more clear Linda, I, and her team were about what was driving his idea, the easier it was for us to get creative about how to satisfy those concerns in other ways. And to do so better than they would have been satisfied by his idea of what to do about them. And of course the more clear *he* was about the "ends behind his means," the easier it was for him to see how well they would be served by the alternatives we presented to him.

■ ■ ■ ■ ■

A Way of Remembering What to Do When

Our thought process is set in motion when we want to attain an end but don't see a good way of going after it. Knowing where we want to go but not knowing how best to get there gives rise to a creative tension that starts a stream of thought. The stream looks something like this:

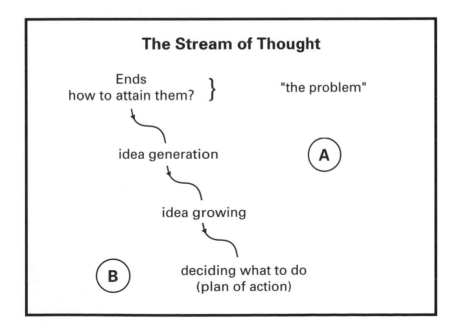

A useful way to think about the difference between the two ways to deal with an idea you don't like — in the one case when it's an idea for you, and in the other when it's something another person wants to do — is as follows.

When the idea is for you, you're at point *A*. You're downstream from a known problem, and you can continue to work your way down toward a plan of action.

When you're dealing with what someone like Jack wants to do, you're meeting him at what is point *B* for him. He got there without you, so you don't know his starting point. To be able to offer alternatives that might be acceptable to him you first have to go upstream with him to discover the ends behind his means.

You may have to go upstream with him more than once — though I didn't need to do this with Jack — if the alternatives you think of after the first trip aren't acceptable to him. This often indicates that you didn't discover the "ends" that really matter to the other person on the first trip.

If you associate the process with the image of a real stream — ideally one you saw and liked — the image can give you a handy way to remember the whys and hows of going upstream.

■ ■ ■ ■ ■

---

* The diagram on the previous page is a simplification of the thought process, which is usually a much more back and forth affair. For example, when you look at the pros and cons of an idea you may discover that the problem you should be working on is not the one you started with, and you thus find yourself back upstream. This can also happen in the idea generation stage.

GOING UPSTREAM:
QUICK REVIEW SUMMARY

The situation: Someone wants to do something. You don't like the idea because if the other person goes ahead with it, that will cause you some grief. You don't have the power to stop the person from going ahead, or have it but don't want to use it that way.

The usual approaches: Try to talk the other person out of it or, if that seems unwise, prepare to suffer in silence. Trying to talk people out of it seldom works. More often it makes them defensive and more determined to go ahead with the idea.

The more productive way: Try to understand *why* the other person wants to do that thing. Then look for other ways for that person to attain those ends, ways that are also more acceptable to you.

In the flow of people's thinking the ends precede the means, and can thus be said to exist "upstream" from them. And it can be said that when you ask people why they want to do something, you are "going upstream" with them.

The Difference Between Going Upstream and Growing an Idea

When you grow an idea you say to the other person: "Here's what *I* think it has going for it, and here's my concern about doing it." Your pros and con(s) give you a blueprint for changing the idea. You can get the blueprint this way when the idea represents something *you* could do about a problem that you posed.

But if the idea represents something the *other person* wants to do, and can do, then you have to take a different tack. To get a blueprint for changing the idea you need to find out what the other person thinks is going for it. But in most cases it isn't productive to say to that person "Let's look at the pros and cons of what you want to do." Saying this is likely to make the other person feel defensive and create an adversarial dynamic between you. And of course if the other person is a testy boss, all you may be told is to get lost.

Creating the right dynamics

You create a much more positive dynamic if you convey an interest in learning more about the problems and concerns the other person's idea is designed to address. You can get the person to talk more about these things by saying something like "May I ask why you'd like to do that?"

You can use other words to draw out the other person, as long as the words and your tone and body language all convey a genuine interest in the other person's situation.

Most people will sense it if you try to fake the interest. You are most likely to set up the right dynamics if you're open to the possibility that what you hear may make *you* change your mind — you may see that what others want to do is the right thing for them to do, and that the right thing for you to do is to live with any grief that causes you.

What You Learn May Also Be News for the Other Person

People aren't always clear about their reasons for wanting to do something. Talking to you about them often helps people to gain a better understanding of what's driving their ideas. This usually makes them more open to other ways of attaining those ends.

A Way of Remembering What to Do When

Associating the stream of "thought" with an image of a real stream — especially one you know and like — can help you remember the whys and hows of "going upstream."

GOING UPSTREAM (vs GROWING IDEAS): AT-A-GLANCE SUMMARY

Situation	Response

Situation

When faced with an idea you don't like, and it is:

A suggestion about what *you* could do about a situation.

Grow it: Say what you think is going for it, talk about your concern(s) ... then tailor or transform.

Something the other person wants to do AND you either don't have the power to block it, or don't want to use it.

Go upstream: Understand the ends the other person is trying to attain by doing that think ... then suggest another way to attain them, a way that's also O.K. with you.

"May I ask why ...?"

7

■ Rule 5: Expose Your Ideas to Criticism ... Before They Are Fully Grown

Why You Need to Do It

We've looked so far at what you can do when you have concerns about other people's ideas — whether these represent things you could do about a situation, or things that they want to do. But what about the concerns others may have about what *you* want to do? You may get to hear some of these but not the rest. Should you actively seek out the latter?

The answer is yes, when what you have in mind involves doing something in a new or different way. And, in that case, it's best to seek out and deal with the concerns in the early stages of the idea's development.

Going out of our way to invite criticism of our ideas is not something that comes naturally to most of us.* Especially when the idea is still young and vulnerable. The tendency is to expose your ideas to attack only if you have to, and to do this only after you've had a

---

* By "inviting criticism" I mean encouraging people to tell you what's *wrong* with your ideas. This is not the dictionary definition of the word "criticism," but it's what most people will take it to mean when you ask for it. (If they went by the dictionary definition their critique would list not only the idea's flaws but also its strengths.)

121

chance to put some armor plate on them. But it's important to do what *doesn't* come naturally, for several reasons:

Doing it will give you a stronger idea. Done right it will increase people's willingness to help you, with that idea and in general. These are the upside reasons for doing it. There's also the other kind of reason — not doing it can cost you a lot. Here's the kind of thing that happens.

THE CASE OF THE USER-FRIENDLY CONTAINER

The background

Patrick is the Marketing Manager for Lube Oils for a European division of a petroleum company. He and his team have developed an easy to use and "drip-free" container for people who like to top up and change the oil in their cars themselves. The new container is an important element in Patrick's plan for increasing their share of this steadily growing segment of their market.

A lot of work went into the development of the new design. This included talking to several groups of typical consumers at the start of the project. Several prototypes were then made and tested for both functionality (were they easy to use and drip-free?) and for appeal (did typical customers like the shape?). Consultants were brought in to design a new logo and label. Discussions were held with their container suppliers to make sure the new design could be produced without any significant increase in costs.

But they didn't discuss the design with the people who ran their container filling plant. Not until after they were done with its development. And then they proudly presented it to Marc, the plant manager, and some of his people.

THE DISCUSSION AND ITS AFTERMATH

"The supplier is ready," Patrick tells them, "to start shipping us these containers in quantity three weeks after we say 'go'."

He explains why it's important to act quickly. Competition is known to be working on a "user-friendly" design, and there is an opportunity to score points with customers by being the first to introduce it.

Marc leans forward and picks up the prototype. He turns it around in his hands as he looks at it.

Just like Marketing, he thinks, to assume that they can design a container all by themselves. And to wait until the last minute to spring it on us, and to then want everything in a hurry.

He puts the prototype back on the table.

"Too bad you didn't show that to us sooner," he says.

"Why, is there something wrong with it?" Patrick asks.

"Yes," Marc says, "two things. The design and your timing. You should know that we have just installed some new high-speed equipment in our plant. To run this thing through the filling lines we would have to shut them down and change several settings. And then do that again to be able to go back to running our regular containers. No way we can do that and meet our production schedule."

Patrick clears his throat.

"Are you sure?" he asks.

"Unfortunately yes," Marc says.

There's a silence. Then Patrick says:

"O.K., so where do we go from here?"

"Nowhere for the next three weeks," Marc says.

What needs to be done, he explains, is for a couple of his people to get together with a few from Patrick's team to rework the design. The two from his side that he has in mind are the ones who know the most about the new filling equipment.

"But these are the very people I can't spare right now," he says. "We are not finished de-bugging the new equipment and are badly behind on our production schedule."

Patrick tries to get Marc to agree to make at least one of those

123

people available sooner. He quotes numbers about the rate of growth of this "Do-It-Yourself" segment of the market, and explains again why it's important to be first out with a user-friendly design.

Marc says if that's true, then the segment is going to be around for a while. In the meantime what about all their other customers, isn't it important to keep them supplied?

Patrick sees that he isn't going to get Marc to change his position so he stops trying — for the moment. After the meeting he goes to see their boss Svend, the division manager. Svend says O.K., I'll talk to Marc. He does and gets Marc to agree to make people available for the redesign starting the following week. Marc is not happy with this decision.

It takes the joint team only two days to rework the design. But prototypes of this modified version have to be made and tested on the filling line. The supplier asks for time to review the modifications and prepare a revised set of cost and delivery quotes.

Patrick loses, by a few weeks, the race to be the first to market a "user friendly" container. And that means more work for him and his people — they have to revise the planned campaign to win market share in the "DIY" segment, because many of its elements were built around the theme of being the leader, the first to respond to those customers' needs.

And Patrick's tactic — getting Svend to pressure Marc into doing something — isn't going to make Marc want to go the extra mile to help Patrick in the future.

■ ■ ■ ■ ■

Don't get boxed in by the organization chart

I could tell you a lot more stories like this one. They all have the same moral: talk to people about what you are thinking of doing. Talk to more than just the usual minimum (those officially responsible for developing an idea or plan plus a few experts from outside this circle, if necessary). And get their reactions to your idea before it's all buttoned up. If you do a lot of work on it before you bounce it off people, you may have to do a lot of that work again afterwards.

And the more you develop an idea before you present it to others, the less flexibility there will be in it for addressing their concerns, and the less room for their ideas.

The question arises, whose concerns — other than those of the usual minimum — should you try to seek out and address? The answer, of course, is the people whose help you're going to need to move the idea forward — especially those who may have to extend themselves to give you the help you need.

There are two ways in which they may have to extend themselves. As discussed earlier, if your plan is innovative — that is, it includes some new or non-standard ways of doing things — then it usually requires implementors to put in more time and effort than they have to for more routine jobs. And it requires the decision-makers who have to approve the plan to take more of a risk — there are more unknowns associated with the new than with the old, including whether it will work at all.

It doesn't take a lot of deep thought to figure out who the key people are whose reactions you need to get. But you may find that going ahead and doing this is not always easy.

■ ■ ■ ■ ■

What Can Keep You From Doing What You Need to Do

I've asked people like Patrick why they didn't do what they, in hindsight, can see they should have done — in his case, talk to Marc sooner than he did. Here's the kinds of things they say:

"It was our responsibility to do something about the situation, so I thought it was up to us to develop the solution."

"We were pushed for time, we didn't want to talk to any more people than we thought we had to."

"I thought we had done a good job of thinking things through, that we had addressed all the key issues."

"I didn't think it was critical. If people had problems with what we were going to propose, we'd find out sooner or later."

All the managers who said such things agreed, again in hind-sight, that these ways of thinking were not productive. So how come smart people like them have to be hit on the head with this fact before they can see it?

The answer is that in any organization of more than a dozen people it's easy to get infected by the mindset that produces these ideas.

When a lot of people are needed for an enterprise it makes sense to organize them into divisions and departments and functions, and to make someone responsible for each area and for each unit in it. Humans aren't the only ones who do something like this — ants do it, bees do it, and hunting wolf packs do it. It's efficient to divide up tasks and give them to the individuals — or groups — who are best equipped to do them. But the system, at least when it's used by humans, is highly vulnerable to a crippling disease.

The name of the disease is "compartmentalization." It makes us see our area of responsibility as distinct and separate from all other areas. It makes us forget that our responsibilities overlap, and that innovation doesn't respect organization charts. It makes us lose sight of the fact that our destinies are closely linked, and that we win or lose together.

It makes us confuse having the responsibility for a task with having to think through, all by ourselves, how best to do it.

It makes us think that tasks for which the responsibility will shift over time — such as new product development — should be run like relay races. One group generates the concept. Another develops it into a feasible product or service. It's then handed over to Production or Marketing or both. And then to Sales. The runner with the baton is supposed to go around the track alone and to interact with the preceding and following runners only in a small hand-off zone.*

The disease also manifests itself in the idea that there is something wrong with reaching across boundaries to draw on the knowledge and ideas of people in a box on the organization chart that's different from yours. This includes the box above you — it's not O.K. to go to your boss and ask for ideas, the boss will think you don't have any of your own. And it's not part of your job to stay in touch with people from other areas, that's an extra-curricular activity, something to be done only when you have time to spare from your real work.

If you don't innoculate yourself against it the disease can induce a fevered state in which you see yourself as a Lone Ranger in the organization. It's O.K. to have one or two buddies, but other than that you're on your own. And in this fevered state you don't see the costs — to the organization and to your ability to do your job — of thinking and acting that way.

An antidote

How to innoculate yourself? Different things work for different people so you'll have to develop your own shot. One that works for many people is to make it a point to meet informally, every week, with a person from an area with which you normally don't have much contact. You can have lunch with that person, or sit together during a break, or go for a coffee (or beer, or whatever) after work.

What you talk about can be strictly business, or things not related to work, or both. Start with someone from a group that you most tend to think of as "them." Two such meetings a week are more than twice as effective as one. But whether it's one or two — or more — to benefit from this activity you have to do it regularly. Like a diet or exercise regimen, it doesn't do much for you if you do it only once in a while.

---

* Companies in which innovation prospers are aware of the dangers of this way of thinking. Many that I know of do things to make all the other runners stay in touch with the one that has the baton, all the way around the track.

127

Your boss and others more senior to you can, in some cases, be good allies in your fight against "compartmental" ways of thinking and acting. The higher they are in the organization the more clearly they can see the big picture and the need for teamwork that transcends boundaries. So they will help you to create time and space for you and people from other "boxes" to put your heads together.

But not all of them will do this. Those who are insecure about their power often seek to bolster it by making themselves the main channel for the flow of information and ideas into and out of their territory. Other channels, such as the ones you establish, are seen as threats to that monopoly.

If you have such a boss you have a problem — you still have to talk about your plans to people from other areas, but you can't expect your boss to bless the activity. But though your boss may not love it, he or she can't come down too hard on you for doing it. After all you are doing it for the right reasons — to make sure your plan is a strong one and that it will move forward smoothly. Just don't put yourself in the position of having to do it after you've asked if you should and been told no (in so many words or with strong hints). So don't ask. And keep in mind that in such situations it is, as one manager put it, "easier to ask for forgiveness than permission." *

■ ■ ■ ■ ■

Doing It Well

O.K., you decide you're going to talk to more people than you normally would about your ideas, find out if they have any concerns about them. What can you do to make the exercise productive?

There are two things that help. One is getting into and maintaining the right frame of mind in your discussions. The other is "know-how" — knowing how to respond effectively to people's criticism of your ideas.

---

* Quoted from the video "Intrapreneuring," by Gifford Pinchot III.

Creating and maintaining the right frame of mind

Criticism can make you feel defensive, even when it's something you've invited. You're especially susceptible here because the criticism is directed at an idea or plan that you hope to see implemented, that represents means for doing your job in an innovative way. And it won't help that most people don't know how to talk about an idea's shortcomings in a way that's easy to hear, that doesn't push your ego agenda buttons.

Whatever the reason, if you get defensive it will be hard to do a good job of listening and responding to the criticism, and of getting people to help you fix the problems they identify. When you become defensive you lose your focus. You do things that are driven more by the need to protect your idea or your ego than by the needs of the task at hand.

You've seen earlier that one of the things you can do to keep your balance is to keep an eye on the "temperature under your collar." Here are some other things you can do in the kind of situation we are talking about here.

Remember it's your show

This is something you're doing for solidly selfish (albeit win-win) reasons. You're inviting the criticism because:

- *You want to use the other person's perspective and knowledge to spot possible flaws in your plan — things you overlooked or that were hard to see from where you sit.*

- *You want to use the occasion to increase the other person's willingness to help you move your plan or idea forward.*

You also need to remember that this is *not* an occasion in which you are required to defend your idea. Your objective is not to get the other person to accept or approve the idea as it stands. You've made it clear that you are asking for comments on a work in progress.

129

You know all this when you start the discussion. But how to remember it when you get the criticism you asked for? Here are two things that will help.

Make a mental cue-card

It helps to have a way to quickly remind yourself that it's your show, without having to remember what's been said above to explain why this is the case. In the heat of battle you don't have time to stop and think about such things.

What you can do is to create a mental "cue-card" you can show to yourself whenever you find yourself slipping into a defensive posture. You don't want a lot of words on the "card" — it takes time to read them. The message you want it to convey can be given much more quickly by an image — of a symbol or analogy that stands for the occasion and your objectives in it. You can grasp the meaning of such images instantly, without needing to have them spelled out in so many words.

You can, for example, think of what you are doing as taking the other person for a test-drive or shake-down cruise on a prototype car or ship you've invented. Or as getting people to try out a workshop model of a golf club or racquet you've designed. Or as asking people to sample a new stew you're cooking and tell you if it's missing something. Whatever.

The image on your mental cue-card can be any picture or symbol associated with the metaphor you pick.

Choose a metaphor that:

- *Feels apt* — It captures the essence, for you, of the situation and your objectives in it.

- *Is appealing* — You like it, think it's grabby. The more you like it the more easily it will become a "cue-card" that shows itself to you, automatically, when you need it.

130

- *Reminds you it's your show* — You're in charge. You're the one taking the other person on a "test ride." And because it's your show, the other person is doing you a favor by coming along. You are, in effect, borrowing the other person's mind for the occasion.

■ Know when to show yourself the card

When should you flash the "cue-card" at yourself? Which is the same as asking: how do you know when you are being — or are about to be —defensive?

You can, of course, keep an eye on the "temperature under your collar." But it's possible to stay cool and still act defensively. So here are two other things to watch for in the kind of situation we're talking about here.

Both have to do with how you respond to the criticism you're given. You are being defensive if you find yourself trying to counter rather than work with the issues and concerns someone raises. The two most common ways of doing this are:

- *Minimizing the concern* — Suggesting that it isn't as important as the other person thinks it is. You may do this without giving any reason for your opinion, or giving ones that aren't convincing. When they are minimizing, people say things like:

  "Don't worry, things will work out O.K."
     or,
  "It's not going to mean that much extra work for your people."
     or,
  "I don't think the customer will be able to tell the difference."

- *Offsetting it* — This is a more indirect way of countering a concern. You don't talk about the concern, you talk instead about the virtues of your plan or idea. You hope that the other person will no longer have the concern if you make it clear that the

idea's plusses are a lot more weighty than it is.*
You might, for example, say:

> "Well yes, that's a good point, but let's not forget what this
> idea is going to do for us

(And then go on to repeat what you've already said about its
virtues, plus add any others that come to mind.)

You rarely get someone to drop a concern by countering it. What
you will succeed in doing is to get into an argument about the
concern's validity or importance. Or to spur the other person to look
for more flaws in your idea and use them in a tit-for-tat exchange —
tell me my concern isn't legitimate and I'll tell you why your idea
isn't either.

Or you may succeed in getting the other person to stop talking
about the concern, not because that person is convinced it isn't important, but is convinced that you are not going to deal with it.

So when you find yourself trying to counter someone's criticism
in either of these two ways, show yourself that cue-card and take a
more productive approach. How you can do this is described next.

How to deal with the concerns

The most effective way of responding to a concern depends on
which of three types it is. The three are:

A. *Those that are based on a misunderstanding. The other person
doesn't fully grasp what your idea is or what it is designed to accomplish, or lacks some information about the situation. You can resolve
such concerns by providing clarification.*

B. *Those that require problem-solving. You or the other person —
or others — need to find solutions for the problems represented by*

---

* It's appropriate to weigh the pros of an idea against its cons when it is time to
decide whether to accept or reject it as it stands. That, of course, is not the case
here.

the concern.

C. ***Those that you need to listen to and acknowledge,*** *but that you don't need to try to resolve because you can't change the circumstances that cause them, or because there's not much to be gained from the effort that would be needed to address them.*

   What you often can *do about such concerns is to make it easier for the other person to live with them.*

Here's an example that illustrates these types of concerns. It also illustrates that to get the most out of such discussions you need to make use of what you know about growing ideas, managing the ego agenda, doing hands-on listening, and going "upstream."

THE BACKGROUND FOR THE DISCUSSIONS

Ellen is a marketing manager who works for the credit card division of a financial services company. She recently ran a "brainstorming" session to generate new premium card concepts. The session included people from several other functions. Ellen got several ideas from the session that look promising and that she intends to test with panels of potential customers. But first she wants to review these ideas with her boss and with colleagues from other functions who in some cases are managers of the people who were in the session.

What will follow are discussions Ellen has about one of the ideas, first with her boss Susan, and then with Jimmy, the head of Customer Service. She'll be talking to them about a concept for a premium card aimed primarily at people who are self-employed or who run small businesses.

One feature of the card is an interest rate, for balances above a certain amount, that is comparable to bank business loan rates. This is to encourage holders to use the card for business charges, and to think of it as a tool for managing their cash-flow needs at a reasonable cost.

Another feature is that the card would give holders access to the equivalent of an airline "club lounge" for people who fly business or first class. Not a place you can walk into physically, but a "virtual" lounge you enter via your computer terminal or telephone or both. Services provided by the lounge could include:

- business news and tips, including summaries of recent changes in tax laws of interest to this group of customers;

- access to a system that would scan and list the lowest airline fare available for a given customer itinerary;

- previous day's closing prices for a customer's selection of stocks plus, if desired, the value of a given portfolio of those stocks;

- access to a live Customer Service representative.

THE DISCUSSION WITH SUSAN

Ellen describes the idea to Susan.

C O N C E R N   T Y P E   A

Susan says "A lot of small business owners don't make good credit risks. Do you really want to give them this card with its high credit line?"

"Good question," Ellen says. "It's one we discussed at the session. The idea is not to give the card to everyone in the segment, only to those who qualify for it by having a certain level of household income."

"Then I don't have that concern," Susan says, but there are some other aspects of this concept that need work. As you described it, the lounge and its services would be available to all card holders. If so this will prob-

C
O
N
C
E
R
N

T
Y
P
E

B

ably be a high annual fee card, which I think is going to scare away those in this segment who care more about getting value for their money than for the prestige of belonging to a club. They won't look past the fee to the aspects of the card that should appeal to them."

"You're making me think," Ellen says, "that instead of making it like the kind of airline club you have to pay a fee to get into, we should make it like the ones for which you qualify by flying a lot."

"Or," says Susan, "what if you make it a two-tier thing. Every card holder gets access to the lounge, but only to the part that provides the services that we can provide at low cost. You get access to the part that provides the higher cost services — such as the more personalized ones — only if you maintain a certain level of usage."

"I like that better," Ellen says, "you get something just for accepting the card, you get more if you use it. What were the other things that you thought needed more work?"

C
O
N
C
E
R
N

T
Y
P
E

B†

"Just one thing," Susan says, "and I'm sure it's a concern you share. I'm not worried about the technical side of this lounge idea ... you'll find out soon if it can be done in a cost effective way. But the weak link is going to be the people part. Are the folks in Operations and Customer Service going to be able and willing to execute this thing well? That's what it will take to make this concept fly, and to keep our card holders once our competitors start offering clones."

"I agree," says Ellen. "I mentioned we had people in the session from both those areas as well as from other

---

Type A: Provide Clarification; B: Problem-Solve; C: Understand & Acknowledge

† It could be argued that this is a type A concern because Ellen dealt with it by explaining what she plans to do about it. But this hasn't made the concern go away, just reassured Susan that Ellen is going to work on it and recognizes its importance.

<table>
<tr><td>

T
Y
P
E

B

c
o
n
t.

</td><td>

functions. We'll continue to consult with them as we develop the concept. My follow-up plan is to have my team look into the technical feasibility and do an analysis of the profit potential of the product, while I focus on the people issues. I was going to talk first to Jimmy in Customer Service."

"Good," says Susan.

</td></tr>
</table>

■ ■ ■ ■ ■

You invite criticism of an idea to make the idea stronger and to create "buy-in" for it. But you seldom create all the buy-in you need in one interaction.

Ellen has made a good start at getting her boss on board. But so far Susan has said yes only to spending some time and effort to explore the feasibility and potential of the new card concept. Ellen will have to continue to keep her boss involved as the project proceeds. How often she does this and what she tries to get out of the discussions depends on what kind of boss Susan is.

Some bosses have a lot of time for their subordinates, others don't. Some like to be involved in idea generation and development, others don't — they'll tell you what's wrong with your idea and leave it to you to fix it. Some bosses don't mind being asked to comment on ideas that are not fully formed and thought out, others have time only for ones that at the very least look all buttoned-up.

Ellen got several things from her discussion with Susan:

- *She got an idea for addressing one of her boss's concerns (make the lounge a two-tier thing, access to the upper tier depends on usage).*

- *The concerns Susan expressed — including those she expects Ellen to work on later — are, in effect, her approval criteria for the project. So Ellen walked away with an understanding of what she needs to build into the concept if she wants her boss to approve the final product.*

136

- She also got Susan's approval for her follow-up plan. This will contribute to Susan's sense of ownership in the idea. People acquire this sense not only through the contributions that help you grow your idea, but also through ones that help you think about the process you use to develop it.

Ellen was able to get these things out of the discussion because she didn't get defensive, and she kept her ego agenda in check. And so she didn't fight Susan's concerns, she worked with them. And she actively drew them out (as when she reminded Susan about something she had said earlier — that she had more than one "other" concern).

■ ■ ■ ■ ■

The Discussion with Jimmy

Jimmy was not in the "brainstorming" session, though two of his people were. Ellen thanks him for making them available and briefly tells him about the several ideas that came out of the session. She then describes in more detail the one she wants to discuss with him first.

"The part of the concept that I most want to get your comments about," she goes on to say, "is the virtual lounge. A part of that is the card holder being able to "talk," in real time, to someone in Customer Service, via the phone or their computer. We talked in the session about the importance of making this a positive experience for the customer. Someone wished we could assign it a dedicated team of reps selected from our top performers. I'd love that, but I thought you might have some concerns about it."

T
Y
P
E

B

Jimmy says, "Well you were right. Other people in marketing also want my best people to focus on their customers. But none of you would like it if I played favorites, if I assigned more good performers to one product than to another. I also wouldn't want to create an elite

137

B | group in my area, not good for the morale of the rest. And I have to say that all the reps are capable of giving good service, though some give it more consistently than others."

"I can't argue with those concerns," Ellen says, "I'd have the same ones in your place."

Ellen can't see how the idea of the dedicated team could be tailored to make it acceptable to Jimmy. It will have to be transformed. So she takes herself "upstream."

"Let's forget about the elite dedicated team," she says, "that's just one way to go after something. It's the 'something' that's important to me. And what is that, why did the idea of the team appeal to me?"

She thinks about it for a few seconds.

"I guess the main reason," she says, "is that by creating a dedicated team you are saying to the people on it 'this is a special set of customers, they're good for our bottom line'. And so people give them special attention."

"If that's what you're after," says Jimmy, "I can see a different way to get it. Right now people who answer calls don't have a way to tell whether the caller is one of our best customers or one of the worst. Sure they call up information about the account on their screens, but they'd have to review the account's entire history with us to know if it's a five- or a zero-star customer. Besides, that's a marketing decision. But if you product managers developed the criteria we could have the system produce a rating."

"So," says Ellen, "one of the first things your people would see on the screen is this star rating, maybe presented in an attention getting way."

"That's right," says Jimmy, "except that I think we should identify only the five-star customer, don't rank the rest. We want to give some people our best service, but we don't want to give anyone poor service."

"Also makes it simpler to do," says Ellen. "What if the system

Type A: Provide Clarification; B: Problem-Solve, C; Understand & Acknowledge also reminds reps, if the caller is a lounge member, to say something like 'welcome to our executive lounge'?"

"Sure," says Jimmy, "that would be O.K."

"Any other comments," Ellen asks, "either about this whole lounge idea or about the overall product concept?"

"No, not really," Jimmy says.

But something in the way he says this makes Ellen think that there is something that's bothering him.

"May not be real," she says, "but I'd still like to hear it."

T Y P E

C

"It's not something we can do much about," Jimmy says, "and it's not about this concept but about any new product. When it's first introduced we're expected to handle it with existing staff. It's a trial period, we can't say how much work it's going to mean for us in the long run, so we have to wait before we can put in for more staff. Makes sense, but it means that in this interim period everyone is extra busy."

"I see," Ellen says, "it's an aspect of product introduction that I wasn't aware of. And I guess you're right, it's something you have to live with. I don't see how we'd justify a request to change the policy."

"Yeah, I know," Jimmy says.

"Doesn't mean though," Ellen says, "that Marketing can't find a creative way to say thanks, to show that we appreciate what your people have to do to get new products off the ground."

"That would help," Jimmy says.

■ ■ ■ ■ ■

In her discussion with her boss Ellen was looking for Susan's comments about any part of the new card concept. But she talked to Jimmy first about the part of the idea that she thought was most relevant to him. Her primary objective was to hear about and work on concerns related to his area of responsibility and expertise. But though she began by talking about that part she *didn't limit the discussion to it. Before they were done she asked for comments about the overall concept. There are two reasons for doing this:*

- *Aspects of your idea other than those you think are relevant can create problems in the other person's area.*

- *People often have useful things to say about aspects of an idea that don't fall into their areas of responsibility or expertise.*

In this discussion Ellen did some hands-on listening and went "upstream," but what she did represents ways of applying these concepts that are different from the ones you saw before.

Earlier, you saw the principle of "going upstream" applied in a situation in which you have concerns about what someone else wants to do ("... put five of your people on my floor ...").

What the other person wants to do represents means for attaining certain ends. You go "upstream" to uncover what those ends are. Once you do, you can suggest other ways to attain them, ways that are also acceptable to you.

In Ellen's case the situation was reversed. She was the one who would have liked to do something that raised concerns for Jimmy. So she took herself "upstream" to clarify, for herself and for Jimmy, why she wanted to do something like that. She also made it clear to him that it was this end that mattered to her, and not the means. This opened the door to finding a way to give her what she wanted without creating problems for Jimmy.

Ellen also listened in a hands-on way, though here she did it to dig out not an idea but a concern.

As with their ideas, people don't always put all their concerns on the table when you ask for them. They may withhold them because they think that not much can be done about them. Or because they think you won't like hearing them. Subordinates, especially, will be very careful about what they say if they think you'll equate criticism of your ideas with lack of commitment to your goals, or with disloyalty to you.

When to dig

How do you know when to dig for concerns? The indicators are in the response you get when you ask for them — the words used, and the tone of voice and body language that accompanies them. You know the kind of thing I mean:

"Any concerns?" you ask.

"Not really," the other person says. With a sigh or a shrug.

Or, after you explain an idea you like to a group of subordinates, you ask:

"Think we should go ahead with this?"

"Sure," says one, with zero enthusiasm.

"If that's what you want," says another.

The others don't say anything but avoid looking you in the eyes.

It's not hard to spot the signs of unvoiced concerns, if you look for them.

■ ■ ■ ■ ■

EXPOSING YOUR IDEAS TO CRITICISM – THE PRACTICE

What's in this section:

- A Perspective Note.
- A Practice Note.
- A Quick Review Summary.

Perspective Note

The last two chapters have focussed on how to manage two situations in which there is potential for conflict: one in which others want to do something you would rather they didn't do, and one in which they have concerns about what you want to do.

You've seen that if you manage these situations the right way, you not only avoid the conflict but create positive outcomes. In looking at the details of how to do this, it's easy to lose sight of the bigger picture, of your larger objective. A reminder of that objective and the part all the rules play in helping you to accomplish it is provided, in diagrammatic form, on the next page.

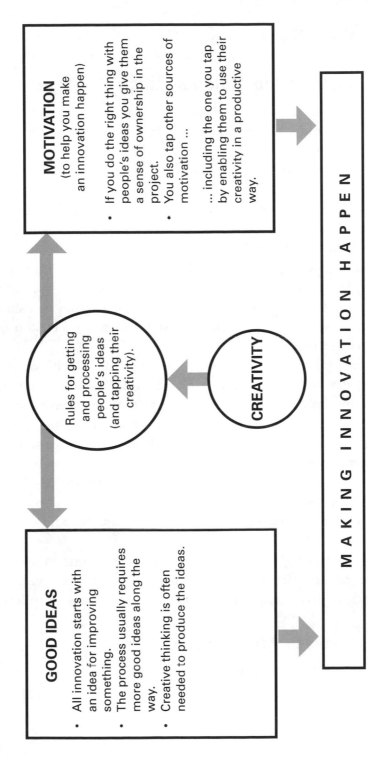

MOTIVATION
(to help you make an innovation happen)

- If you do the right thing with people's ideas you give them a sense of ownership in the project.
- You also tap other sources of motivation ...

... including the one you tap by enabling them to use their creativity in a productive way.

GOOD IDEAS

- All innovation starts with an idea for improving something.
- The process usually requires more good ideas along the way.
- Creative thinking is often needed to produce the ideas.

Rules for getting and processing people's ideas (and tapping their creativity).

CREATIVITY

M A K I N G   I N N O V A T I O N   H A P P E N

A WAY TO THINK ABOUT WHAT THE RULES DO FOR YOU

Practice Note

Think about no more than 3 things at a time

Ellen, in her discussions with her boss and with Jimmy, did a lot of things. She did the things described in this chapter. She also used principles associated with the rules described earlier.

All that may feel like too many things to have to remember when you're talking to someone. And they would be, if you had to think about them all — it would be like trying to think of all the things you knew about hitting a good tennis or golf shot while you were hitting one in an important match.

Most golf pros say you should have no more than three swing thoughts in your head when you are out on the course. This doesn't mean there are only three things you need to do to hit good shots in a variety of situations. Just that you don't want to focus on more than three of them at any one time.

A limit of three thoughts is also a good one to go with when you use the rules described in this book. Ellen, for example, may have had in mind only two thoughts: an image that helped her maintain the right frame of mind, and the thought that she was going to be dealing with three kinds of concerns. All the other things she did — avoid countering concerns, listen for them in a hands-on way, grow ideas, go "upstream" — were likely done on automatic pilot. She had incorporated them into her "swing" on other occasions, so they were not things she needed to attend to consciously in these discussions.

The three thought limit is an especially good one to use when you first start to practice a new rule. You could apply it to your practice of rule 5 (invite criticism) by proceeding in stages, as follows:

Stage 1 — the first few occasions

Focus on doing just two things:

- inviting criticism from people you normally don't include in the development of your plans and ideas;

- keeping in mind an image that helps you to maintain a non-defensive stance.

On these occasions don't worry about what kind of concern you are dealing with or how to respond to it. Just be guided by common sense and your sense of the situation. And if you find yourself using skills associated with other rules that's great, as long as using them wasn't part of your conscious agenda.

Stage 2 — the next few occasions

Continue to work on getting into and maintaining a non-defensive stance. Focus on doing the following:

- keeping in mind the two ways of countering instead of working with the criticism you get (minimizing someone's concern about your idea, or countering it by talking about the idea's strong points);

- Backing off when you find yourself doing either of these two things.

Again, don't worry about any other aspects of your engagement process, do what comes "naturally."

Stage 3 — subsequent occasions

Look now at what you do with people's concerns. Focus on:

- identifying the kind of concern you're dealing with (and whether to provide clarification, problem-solve, or only understand & acknowledge);

- looking for signs of unspoken concerns and digging them out.

145

■ ■ ■ ■ ■

You don't, of course, have to proceed as outlined above. You may feel ready to jump into stage 3. Or feel that you are ready to start using rule 5 without having to think consciously about any aspects of it. All you need to do before the first few times you use it is to glance at the quick review summary.

EXPOSING YOUR IDEAS TO CRITICISM: QUICK REVIEW SUMMARY

Why You Need to Do It

You expose your ideas to criticism to make them stronger, and to increase people's willingness to help you move them forward. You also do it to avoid costly delays, rework, and hard feelings.

It's best to invite critcism of a plan or idea in the early stages of its development. The less developed it is the easier to modify it to take care of others' concerns about it, and the more room in it for their ideas.

Who to invite comments from? Key people among those whose help you'll need to move an idea forward, especially those who may have to extend themselves to give you that help (by approving it or implementing it).

What Can Keep You From Talking to Enough People

In any organization of more than a dozen people it's easy to get infected by a "compartmental" way of thinking and acting. You have to find a way of inoculating yourself against this disease.

(For example, by making it a point to get together with people from other "boxes," more regularly and frequently than you do normally.)

Doing It Well

Making the exercise productive involves two things: maintaining a non-defensive frame of mind, and knowing how to deal with people's concerns.

Ways of doing these things are summarized on the next page.

EXPOSING YOUR IDEAS TO CRITICISM: AT-A-GLANCE SUMMARY OF THE HOW

Dealing with the concerns

Type of concern	Way to respond
Is based on a misunderstanding	Clarify idea or situation it's designed to address
Requires problem-solving	Find a way to address the concern that's acceptable to you and to the other person
Needs acknowledge-ment but not problem-solving	Make sure you understand it, show empathy, and if you can, make it easier for the other to live with it

Maintaining a non-defensive stance

Remember it's your show

Make a mental cue-card
An image related to a metaphor that:

- Feels apt
- Is appealing
- Reminds you it's your show

Know when to show yourself the card
You are being defensive if you try to counter others' concerns ... the two most common ways of doing this are:

- Minimizing them
- Trying to offset them by selling your idea's strong points

8

■ Rule 6: Involve People, But Keep Them Off Your Decision Turf

It's Another Thing the Rules Help You Do

The rules described in the previous chapters give you the tools you need to solve a problem most people face when they try to involve others in the development of their plans to make an innovation happen.

Many of the managers I talk to worry that the involvement will open the door to people telling them how to do their job. They think that by including others in the thinking they do to develop their plans they are practicing participative management, which they equate with making decisions by consensus or majority vote. And this is a thought that makes them uncomfortable.

It's a legitimate worry. There may be times when it's necessary to operate by consensus — such as when you are part of a committee or task force whose members are all equally responsible for making something happen. But if you're the one accountable for the results you get from an action plan then you naturally want to retain, as much as possible, the right to decide what goes in it.

Here's how the use of the rules helps you to preserve this right.

The two ways to create ownership and commitment

There are two things you can do to give people a sense of owner-ship in a plan.

One is to give them a vote or veto in the decisions you have to make during its development (about such things as what the plan's objectives should be, or which of several ideas for attaining them you should include in the plan).

The second thing you can do is to help people contribute useful ideas to your plan. (This is what the rules enable you to do.)

The better you are at doing the second thing, the less you need to rely on the first to give people ownership in your plan.

Say, for example, that you're talking to two people from another department. One of them has an idea. She's a bit apologetic about it because she doesn't think it's a good one. You involve them both in growing the idea into some-thing that's both appealing and practical. So who owns the finished product? The answer, of course, is that it be-longs to all three of you.

Say further that in the same discussion you draw out and develop two more of their ideas. You now have three, but there's room in your plan for only one of those ideas. You don't have to give the others a vote about which one goes in the plan. It doesn't diminish their sense of having made a useful contribution to your plan if *you* make that decision, because they both own a piece of all three ideas.

Giving people a piece of ownership in a plan by helping them to make useful contributions to it is a better option than doing it by giving them votes or vetoes in the decisions you make during its development. There are two reasons for this. One, of course, is that the first way helps preserve your right to decide what goes in your plan. The other is that it leads to greater commitment to help you with your plan, commitment that goes beyond that which comes from a sense of ownership alone.

Here are some other things you can do to preserve your right to make the decisions you feel you should make.

Keeping Bosses Off Your Decision Turf

The people most likely to trespass on your "right to decide" turf are the ones above you in your organization chart. Your domain is part of their duchy so they feel free to invite themselves into your part of it. Two common ways of doing this are:

- by pushing you to include their ideas in your plan, ideas you wouldn't put in it if it was your decision;

- by vetoing ideas you want to put in it.
  What can you do about this? Here are some things.

Involve them ... sufficiently ... in the right activity

The process of developing a plan to make an innovation happen includes four activities*:

A. *Defining the scope.* This is about identifying and prioritizing the problems and opportunities you want the plan to address. It's also about defining how you will measure success, and clarifying the resource or other constraints the plan must live with.

B. *Generating ideas.* How are you going to attack the problems and opportunities identified in the first activity?

It's best to think of what you need to do to answer this ques-

---

* You don't always go through these activities in a strictly sequential fashion. To produce an effective plan you often have to go back and forth between them.

151

tion as consisting of two distinct steps. In the first — this one — you get raw material, not finished product.

You want to think of this as an activity that's distinct from what you do in the second step (idea growing) because this gives you the option of involving different kinds and numbers of people in the two activities.

C. *Growing ideas.* Converting the raw material into "good" ideas that are candidates for inclusion in your action plan.

D. *Deciding what to do.* Outlining the action plan.

Bosses often barge into the last activity — the one in which you most want to retain your decision rights — because you didn't involve them sufficiently in the first three, especially activity A. That's the one in which you clarify the things with which they are — or should be — most concerned.

If you don't involve them enough in the first three activities they may barge into the last one simply because they want to feel involved in the innovation you are trying to make happen. If you don't direct that involvement you may get it where you least want it.

But they may also barge into activity D (Deciding what to do) because they aren't sure you fully understand what they think are the key goals and priorities of your project. Telling you what to put in your action plan is a way of making sure it meets their objectives.

So make sure you involve the boss enough in the process, especially in activity A (Defining the scope). *The "enough" has less to do with the amount of time you spend talking to your boss and more to do with the quality of the interaction.* How hard did you work to make sure you understood what was important to your boss? Did you help your boss to think of not just the obvious issues and opportunities but a few non-obvious ones as well? How well did you listen for and draw out the wishes and concerns your boss may have about the innovation?

The more reassured a boss feels that you understand these things, the less likely he or she is to impose ideas on you. And the more clearly you understand them the more likely you are to develop ideas that won't get vetoed.

Tailor the approach to fit the boss

Some bosses will be happy to help you define the scope of your plan. Others won't give you much help — they'll take the view that you ought to know what's important to them without their having to spell it out for you. Often the only way to get these bosses to tell you what you want to know is to give them an idea to react to. If you know or suspect that this is the case, you can try the following tack:

> Take a first cut at activities B and C (idea generation and growing).
>
> Don't spend too much time on them or involve a lot of other people, yet.
>
> Give the boss a few ideas to react to.
>
> If the boss doesn't tear them apart, great — your guess about how to define the scope was right.
>
> If the boss *does* tear the ideas apart, also great because in the process the boss can't help giving you information about what's important to him or her.
>
> You may have to do this more than once. Makes extra work for you but nowhere near as much as if you do all you need to do to develop what you think is a good action plan, and then have the boss tell you, in effect, to go back to the drawing board.

If they insist, take them upstream

No matter how good a job you do of understanding what's important to the people above you, there will be times when they try to push unwelcome ideas on you anyway. You already know how to deal with such ideas. Here's a quick review.

How you deal with a boss's unwelcome ideas depends on how they are presented to you. If they are presented as suggestions — "just ideas," not prescriptions you're expected to follow — then you can say "Here's what I think is going for that idea, here's the problem I have with it." And then grow the idea, with or without the boss's help.

But if it's more than a suggestion, if the boss is saying "Do it this way" — or has not said that but made it clear he or she would really like you to make it a part of your plan — then the boss isn't interested in hearing what you like or don't like about the idea. The more productive thing for you to do here is to go "upstream." Try to understand the reasons why the boss wants you to do that thing in that way. Once you know that you can suggest other ways of attaining those ends, ways that are also O.K. with you.

Keep in mind that people — including bosses — often get enamored of an idea because it represents a way of satisfying an important wish or concern, but one that they aren't fully aware they have. When you take them upstream from their idea, you often make not just you but also them more aware of what's important to them. This usually makes them receptive to any alternative means you suggest. (Of course, becoming more clear about what they think is important may make you see that including their idea in your plan isn't such a bad thing to do after all.)

If You Give People Votes, Don't Get Locked Into the Majority Rule

Say you've asked a dozen people to come to a meeting. You want them to generate ideas. You also want them to help you grow some of those ideas. The group comes up with twenty-five ideas, which can be clustered into seven concepts. You think there's enough time left to grow three of these concepts.

You'd like to involve the group in helping you decide which three of the seven to work on further in this meeting. You give each person two votes, only one of which can be cast for a person's own ideas.

Two of the concepts get six votes. One gets five. No other concept gets more than three. One gets only two votes, but both of the people who picked it are very excited about it. So how do you proceed from here?

Most managers would feel bound, at this point, to go with the three concepts that got the most votes. And if that's what they did, the other group members would go along with the decision. After all, isn't that what you're supposed to do if you ask people to vote — go with whatever or whoever gets the largest number of votes?

Yes, perhaps in the world of politics. But it isn't the optimum thing to do if you're trying to develop good ideas and get people behind them. In this case you don't want to ignore what the numbers say, but you don't want to make them the only criteria you use to decide how to proceed. Here's why:

- *You're not trying to determine, in this activity, which are the "best" concepts, only* which ones people most want to work on first. *They may in fact pick the "worst" ideas to go with first, if they know that these are often the ones that lead to the "best" finished product.*

- *Remember you want the finished product to be not just useful but also something about which people feel positively, especially if they are the ones who will implement the idea, and the quality of the execution matters. So how people* feel *about the items they vote for is a weighting factor you need to take into account. (Twelve lukewarm votes may count for less than three passionate ones.)*

- *You are not asking people to help you decide which are the "best" candidates for inclusion in your action plan. So why risk making people feel like "losers" either because one of their ideas didn't get the most votes, or because they didn't vote for the "winners"?*

Just because an idea is not selected for more work right then doesn't mean you won't grow it later, or that it won't turn out to be the one that leads to the most exciting finished product. So it isn't appropriate for people to turn the vote into a contest to see whose ideas "win." You can underline this point by de-emphasizing the importance of the numbers.

You want to de-emphasize the numbers, but you don't want to ignore them either. So in the above example you could decide to work on the two concepts that got the most votes, plus the one that got only two but with a lot of feeling attached to them.

If you are not going to go strictly by the numbers, let people know this before they vote. You're asking them to play a game that's different from the one most will think it is, if you don't tell them otherwise. People like to know the rules of a game before they start playing it.

Be Clear About Which Turf You Want to Protect

Say you're talking to two subordinates about how to provide better service to a set of customers. Together, you develop two ideas (A & B) that are acceptable to you. This means that they have, in your mind, crossed the line that separates concepts you consider "just ideas" from those you think are candidates for action.

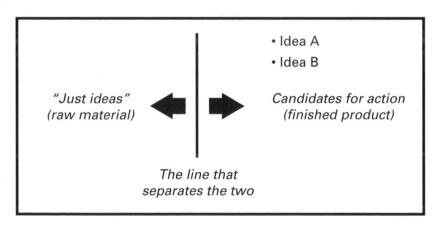

You have the resources to implement only one of the two ideas. Who should decide which one to go with, you or the subordinates?

I've asked a lot of managers what typically happens in a situation like this. The answer I always get is "The boss decides, of course."

"Why?" I ask.

"Well," they say, "because that decision belongs to the boss."

But should it?

You, as the boss, can say to your subordinates, "Look, I own the line. I — and I alone — decide whether an idea belongs on one side of it or the other."

Fair enough, it's your neck if things don't work out. But once you've decided that ideas A and B are both on the actionable side of the line, why must you always *also* decide which one to go with?

What if you don't have any strong preference for either A or B, but B appeals a lot more to both subordinates? (Or to one, with the other feeling as you do, it could be a coin toss.) In this case you're likely to get better execution of the idea if you let them make the decision.

Even if none of the three of you is strongly in favor of one idea, you may still want to let them make the decision if you think this will add to their sense of empowerment and that this, in turn, will have a positive impact on their performance.

▪ ▪ ▪ ▪ ▪

The general principle is this: To determine which decisions you ought to make be guided not just by whether you are a boss or a subordinate but also by the other specifics of the situation. You may want to let go some decisions you're "supposed" to make as a boss. And you may want to fight for the right to make some you're not "supposed" to make because you are a subordinate.

There's a corollary of the principle: To avoid unnecessary turf fights when you're developing a plan of action, keep in mind who thinks which decisions belong to them.

Activity	Decision(s) about	Who thinks decision should belong to them
A. Defining the scope	What are the key problems, oppty's, success measures, & constraints	Bosses
B. Generating ideas	What kinds of ideas to generate? Which ideas to grow first?	Person(s) who invite the ideas Ditto (but usually feel O.K. giving votes to others)
C. Growing ideas	Which ideas are candidates for action?	Person(s) accountable for making the innovation happen and Experts (esp. for technical ideas)
D. Deciding what to do	What goes in the action plan?	Person(s) accountable for making the innovation happen Bosses

WHO NEEDS TO BE INVOLVED MOST IN WHICH ACTIVITY

INVOLVE PEOPLE, BUT KEEP THEM OFF YOUR DECISION TURF

QUICK REVIEW SUMMARY

There are two ways to create ownership in and commitment to a plan of action:

- give people votes or vetoes in the decisions that need to be made in the plan development process;

- help them to contribute useful ideas to the plan.

Use of the rules in the preceding chapters enables you to take the second path, which is better because it:

- helps you preserve your right to decide what goes in your action plan;

- leads to commitment to help you that goes beyond what you get from a sense of ownership alone.

Keeping bosses off your decision turf

- Involve them ... sufficiently ... in the right activity.

- Tailor the approach to the boss.

- If they insist, take them "upstream."

If you give people votes, don't get locked into the "majority rule"

- If it's about which ideas to grow, don't go strictly by the numbers. (Twelve luke-warm votes may count for less than three passionate ones.)

- Let people know the rules of your voting game.

Be clear about which turf you want to protect

- Be guided not just by whether you're a boss or a subordinate, but also by the other specifics of the situation.

- To avoid unnecessary turf fights, keep in mind who thinks which decision belongs to them (in the plan development process).

9

■ Rule 7: Acknowledge Contributions to Your Thinking

A Few Words Can Say a Lot

You frequently get ideas and insights from other people, but they don't always know they've given you something useful. If you let them know they've done this you get more from the occasion than just an idea. You increase their sense of ownership in that idea, and in any plan into which you incorporate it. And you say something about yourself: that you're big enough to acknowledge your intellectual debts.

There are two ways to acknowledge contributions to your thinking. The usual way is to give people credit for any of their ideas that you include in your plans or reports or recommendations. This is an after-the-fact, public acknowledgement of their contribution to an intellectual product. It's important to do this if you want them to continue to give you that kind of help. But you know this, and you also know how to give this kind of credit. So it's not the kind of acknowledgement I'll talk about here.

I'll talk instead about a way of acknowledging contributions that is more immediate and ongoing, and is something you may not do often enough. It's something that's very simple to do and that, if done consistently, creates a positive interpersonal dynamic between you and others. *It's a way of being,* a stance you take that allows people to see their impact on the way you think about a situation. You acknowledge this impact regardless of whether you ultimately use the idea or insight it produces.

Why the impact isn't obvious to others

Letting people see that they've had an impact on your thinking means letting them know that something they said or did — a comment they made, a question they asked you, a suggestion or piece of information they gave you — added to your understanding of a situation, or added to your stock of ideas for dealing with it. People may be unaware that they've helped you in this way for one or both of two reasons.

One is that only you know for sure that a suggestion or piece of information you're given is an *addition* to what was already in your head when you were given it.

The other reason is that often only you can see that the idea or insight you got was derived from what someone said or did. To get something useful out of a suggestion you sometimes have to tailor or transform it so much that the finished product bears little resemblance to the raw material you were given. If that work was done in your head only you know for sure that the one thing grew out of the other. And when an insight is triggered in your mind, as it often can be, by what someone says in jest or in an aside unrelated to the subject of the discussion, only you can see the connection between the two things.

Barriers

You don't have to do anything complicated to let people know they've made a contribution to your thinking. Just let them know you got a useful thought from something they said or did.

But though what you need to do is simple, to do it consistently you have to be aware of the things that can keep you from doing it. And that can make you do something like the following instead.

Jacques is having lunch with a colleague, Toni. He's been telling her about a customer who a few months ago started complaining a lot more than he used to about the service he's getting from Jacques's group.

"Maybe," Toni says, "that's because his customers began to give *him* a hard time about then. You know, kid kicks dog, dog bites cat."

Jacques has been operating on the assumption that the increase in complaints has something to do with a change he made in the people assigned to the account. He noticed the increase shortly after he made the change. What Toni said makes him wonder if the cause is not that change but some other change in the customer's circumstances. He knows a lot about the customer's situation. Based on what he knows he doesn't think it could be anything to do with the customer's customers. But what about his other suppliers? That could be it!

What he finds himself saying to Toni is:

"Nah, that's not it. I know something about this guy's business. It can't be anything to do with his customers. I think maybe it's something his other suppliers started doing to him."

This response isn't going to make Toni feel great. She's just been told that what she thought was wrong when in fact the essence of it was right, just the details were off. And Jacques makes it sound as if he had the "right answer" all along, which is as it should be because he knows more about the customer than she does.

You couldn't blame Toni for thinking "O.K., if you know it all then you worry about the problem, you don't need any ideas from me or anyone else." And she might be left with the suspicion that perhaps Jacques *didn't* have the right answer all along, perhaps it was what she said that made him think of it, only he isn't big enough to admit it.

Toni's reaction would, of course, be very different if

> Jacques had said:
> "I doubt it's his customers, but you've made me think that maybe it's not anything we're doing, maybe he's re-acting to something someone else started doing to him. It could be his other suppliers. I'll look into that, thanks."

Why did Jacques make the first response and not the second? What could cause you to do something similar in that kind of situation?

Jacques may, of course, have said what he did simply because he had never thought about the consequences of saying that versus something else. But even if you are aware of the consequences, there are three other things that can keep you from making the more productive response.

The first thing

What can most often cause you to *not* acknowledge someone's contribution to your thinking is the same thing that can keep you from acting effectively in other ways — the ego agenda.

It manifests itself here as the need to say "*I* think ..." when it would be more accurate and more productive to say "You made me think ..." The ego agenda can make you equate acknowledging an intellectual debt with acknowledging your lack of smarts — if you were really on the ball you would have thought of that thing on your own, you wouldn't have needed any prompting from the other person. But is this really so? Does letting others see the impact they have on your thinking diminish you in some way in their eyes?

A part of you may say "Of course not." But if you have never consciously thought about the question and convinced yourself the answer is unequivocally "no," then another part of you may not be so sure. When there's a doubt about such things the ego agenda pushes us to do the thing that feels safe, even though it's not the effective thing to do. So let's put the doubt to rest.

It didn't diminish Sir Isaac Newton in anyone's eyes when he said, in a letter to the physicist Robert Hooke, "If I have seen further (than you or Descartes) it is by standing on the shoulders of Giants." By saying this he probably *enhanced* his image with his peers. Accomplished people know that a key to their success is their ability to make good use of other people's ideas, and not just of those they consider giants. They also know that not everyone is big enough to admit this.

A friend who plays drums in a jazz group (on the side, not for a living) has taken lessons from and hung out with some great players. He says they "Wear out recordings by others whose work they admire." They listen to them again and again, soaking up musical ideas — how to phrase something, how to play with a theme, how to make an instrument talk. They call the ability to pick up such ideas "having a great ear."

If acknowledging intellectual debts enhanced rather than diminished Newton's image, if it does the same thing for great musicians and other successful people, then it will also do it for you and me.

The second thing

Sometimes we don't bother to make clear to others that we were led to a thought by what they said because we assume the connection between the two things is obvious. Yes it is, to us, because it was made in our heads. We forget that others didn't see how we went from their "A" to our "B" so the link between the two things isn't obvious to them.

The third thing

We may also not acknowledge someone's contribution to our thinking because we ourselves are not aware of it, at least not at the conscious level. This can happen for one or both of the following reasons.

The first is that what goes on in our heads happens very quickly, and what happened can quickly fade from view. Also, because we tend to focus on the idea or conclusion that is the *end-product* of our thinking, the first thing to fade from view is the thought process that got us to it. What went before it can fade out really fast if some aspect of the end-product is fresh and is accompanied by a "eureka" or "aha" reaction. The stronger this reaction the more our attention gets grabbed by the end-product and the easier it is to lose sight of the thing that made us think of it.

In the earlier example, Jacques may have been done with the thinking that got him to his conclusion — maybe the problem is the customer's other suppliers! — before Toni was done talking. If he got all caught up with that thought he could easily have lost sight of both how Toni led him to it and of the need to acknowledge this.

The second reason we may not see that someone contributed to our thinking is that often there's only a fuzzy, more sensed than seen connection between what someone says and the idea it triggers for us. Here's an example.

You're taking a break during a meeting you called to discuss a new sales campaign.

"Did you see the basketball game on TV last night?" Anthony asks you.

"No I didn't," you say. But someone else did see it and she and Anthony start talking about it.

For some reason the image of a basketball bouncing off the rim of a hoop makes you think that perhaps the previous sales campaign didn't work as well as hoped because it wasn't aimed at the right market segment. The more you think about it the more convinced you are that you are right. You wonder if you are making the same mistakes with some aspects of the campaign you've been talking about in this meeting. You wait impatiently for the break to end so you can discuss this possibility with the others.

The thought you get in such cases is derived from what the other person said by associative or analogical thinking. This makes it hard to see that there is a connection between the two things because it's usually made in a flash and made unconsciously, or at the fringes of awareness. And even if you do see the connection it may not feel like a situation that involves a debt — after all, the other person wasn't deliberately trying to give you an idea.

But the fact that it was an unintentional gift doesn't make the idea any less useful to you. And you wouldn't have got it if the other person hadn't said the thing that spawned it. So there's still a debt involved, though it may be stretching things a bit to call it that. But that's also the reason why its acknowledgment will pay an extra dividend — it will be unexpected and it will feel generous to the other person.

Doing It

What you need to do to acknowledge contributions to your thinking is simple:

If it isn't clear to people that something they gave you *is a useful addition to your thinking,* let them know that.

And if it isn't clear that what you got *was derived from something they said or did,* let them know this also.

As the following examples illustrate, it isn't hard to figure out what to say. They also illustrate how the things we've just talked about can make it hard to remember to say it.

SITUATION A

You're giving your boss a progress report on a program to develop a new software application. You describe a technical problem you've run into. Your boss suggests a way to get around it. It's something you hadn't thought of trying. You think it might work.

Here you need only make clear you got something useful because, if you did, it's obvious you got it from your boss. All you have to say is something like:

"That might do it, thanks"

or,

"Good idea. I'll let you know how it works."

What about the degree of difficulty, in this case, of acknowledging the contribution? On a scale of 1 (easy) to 10 (very hard), I'd give it a 2 if your relationship with your boss is relatively free of ego agenda games. The number would be a lot higher if the situation is one in which it will feel like a defeat to admit you didn't think of the idea yourself.

SITUATION B

You're a V.P. of Manufacturing. You think it would be cost effective to let outside vendors make some of the parts your division makes for your company's line of communications equipment. You've had preliminary talks with a few potential suppliers. You mention what you are thinking of doing to Keith, the head of Purchasing.

"The suppliers you're looking at," he says, "how compatible are their inventory control systems with ours?"

It hadn't occurred to you to look for this compatibility. You've been concentrating on finding out whether the suppliers can make the parts cheaper than you can and at the same time meet your quality standards. You see right away the additional cost benefits of having the compatibility Keith mentioned. Obvious when you think about it, and you should have thought of it yourself.

Keith has no way of knowing that his question made

you think of doing something you hadn't thought of doing. Nor that you think it would be a useful thing to do. You can let him know both these things by saying something like:

"Good question. Should have thought of it myself, but I didn't. Their control system will be part of our selection criteria now. Thanks."

On the same scale of 1 to 10, how easy or hard would it be for *you*, in a similar situation, to keep your balance and acknowledge the contribution?

Keep in mind that there is a booby trap for your ego agenda in this kind of situation. It can be hard to admit that you didn't think of something you feel you should have thought of. Instead of thanking Keith you could easily find yourself saying:

"We'll look at that in due course, but first things first. Won't do us much good if the inventory systems are a perfect match but the supplier can't deliver on cost and quality."

You don't actually say that the point Keith raised is something you had already thought of. But it wouldn't be hard for Keith to get that impression from what you do say.

■ ■ ■ ■ ■

If you scored this one "easy" it means that it won't take you long to make acknowledging contributions a part of the way you are with people. If you scored it "hard" it will take you longer. But perhaps not, if being aware that it could be hard also makes you more aware of your ego agenda and of how others trigger ideas for you.

■ ■ ■ ■ ■

Variations On the Theme

All the situations described so far are ones in which the contributions to your thinking are made in face-to-face discussions, and in

169

which they are acknowledged at the time they are made. But they can both be made in other ways and acknowledged at another time.

The question or comment or suggestion or piece of information that gives you a useful thought can come your way over the telephone, or via e-mail, or by someone sending you a clipping of an item from a newspaper or journal. Regardless of how it's transmitted it may give you your useful thought right away or after a while. (As, for example, when someone gives you an impractical idea. It may not be until two days later, in the shower or on your way to work, that you see how to grow it into something you can use.)

When should you tell people you got a useful thought from something they said or did? In most cases right after you get it, because then you don't have to remember to do it. But right away isn't always the most appropriate time for it. For example:

You and a colleague are making a joint sales call. You're from Sales. Your colleague Kwan is from Technology. You're making a presentation of a new product. About a third of the way through it Kwan gets into the act and asks your customers several questions about their business. Initially you don't appreciate the interruption but quickly realize her questions are good ones. Asking them at that point in the presentation brings home to the customers how the new product would help them to run their business more effectively. This makes them very receptive to the rest of the presentation.

What Kwan did has shown you a way to improve your presentation. She won't be there when you make it to the next group of customers, but her questions will be. You plan to make them a part of your presentation. You don't think it's appropriate to tell her this during this meeting. You'll tell her after it when you are both in your car headed back to the office.

ACKNOWLEDGING CONTRIBUTIONS – REVIEW

What's in this section:

- A Quick Review Summary.

- A Caution.

- At-A-Glance Summary of the how.

QUICK REVIEW SUMMARY

Letting people see that they've made an impact on your thinking doesn't cost you much effort but gives you a high return. It gives others ownership in the idea or insight you got from them, and in any plan into which you incorporate it. And if you do it consistently, it creates a positive interpersonal dynamic between you and them.

Two things contribute to the positive dynamic. You make people feel valued when you tell them they've added something to your understanding of a situation, or to your stock of ideas for dealing with it. And you make it clear to them that you don't let your ego keep you from acknowledging your intellectual debts.

The kind of acknowledgment described here is different from giving people credit for any of their ideas that you include in a plan or report or recommendation. What this rule is about is a way of being, a stance you take that allows people to see the impact they have on your thinking, and to see that in an ongoing way.

How you acknowledge a contribution in any situation is easy to see. But there are things that can keep you from making it a part of the way you are with people. These things are:

- Your ego agenda.

- Forgetting that others can't see how your mind went from what they said or did to the idea or insight you derived from it.

- Losing sight of the connection yourself.

171

The key to overcoming these barriers is to be aware of them. And to keep in mind the benefits of making it a habit to say those few words.

■ ■ ■ ■ ■

THE CAUTION

Telling people that something they said or did gave you an idea is an easy way to increase their sense of ownership in it. And so it can be tempting to pretend that's how you got an idea when this is not the case.

Faking it — saying something like "What you just said made me think ..." and then trotting out an idea you had all along — seldom works. You may fool someone once in a while, but most of the time you won't. People will sense that the two things aren't really connected, and this will cost you in a couple of ways. People will resent your attempt to manipulate them. And your credibility will take a hit.

So send the temptation packing.

ACKNOWLEDGING CONTRIBUTIONS: AT-A-GLANCE SUMMARY OF THE HOW

- If it isn't clear to others that something they gave you *is a useful addition to your thinking*, let them know that.

  And if it isn't clear that what you got *was derived from something they said or did*, let them know this also.

- How you acknowledge the contribution is simple. You can say something like:

  "You just gave me an idea ..."

  or,

  "I hadn't thought of that, I'll look into it. Thanks."

  or,

  "Thanks for that piece of information you sent me, it helped clarify the problem."

- Both the contribution and the acknowledgment can be made in face-to-face discussions, or in other ways.

- In general, let people know you got something useful from them right after you get it, or as soon after that as is possible and appropriate.

10

■ Rule 8: Invite Ideas Only When You're Open to Them

Others Don't Win If You Don't Get Something You Can Use

This final chapter is going to be different from the preceding ones. Here I'm not going to be talking about how to do something, but about why *not* to do something you may be tempted to do. And that is to try to make people think you want their ideas when you don't.

Asking people for their ideas can be a win-win thing to do, if you do it for the right reasons. You win because you get ideas that increase the effectiveness of your plans. And by including their ideas in your plans you increase people's willingness to help you move them forward. What's in it for them is the enhanced sense of self-worth that comes from seeing their ideas valued, which is what you do when you dig out of them something that's useful to you.

The key words here are *useful to you.* For others to win, *you* have to get out of the discussion an idea or insight you think you can use. There's no joy in it for them if this is not the case, because *the extent to which they feel you value their thinking is directly proportional to its perceived utility to you.*

To make the "asking" a win-win thing it helps to know how to draw out, and get the most out of others' ideas. But though necessary this know-how is not enough. You also have to be open to people's ideas. This means, one, that you think it's possible for them to add depth or breadth or freshness to your thinking. And two, that you want this "idea help."

The Temptation

Now if you're *not* open to ideas, why would you bother to invite them? You're not going to get any you like, and that's going to be a downer for the other person — it's no fun to be asked for ideas only to find out the asker has no use for them. And yet I see a lot of smart people doing it anyway, including ones who care about how others feel.

They do it, of course, because they think they can get something *other* than ideas by doing it. And that they can get it without putting people off.

I often see people asking for ideas when they aren't open to them because they think it's a way to build commitment to an idea or relationship. They think this because they buy the basic thesis of this book: You can get to people's hearts through their minds. A way to do this is to make them feel you want and value their ideas.

But if you don't really want the ideas, then by asking for them you're playing a game. It's a very seductive game because it looks like one in which the deck is stacked in your favor — you know what you are up to, the other person doesn't. But in fact the odds are against you. In most cases you'll lose, and you'll lose a lot more than you think because the costs aren't easy to see.

How susceptible are you to the temptation?

How likely are you to be tempted to play the game anyway, despite what I've said so far? Depends on how much you have in common with the people I see playing it.

THE PLAYER'S PROFILE

You're likely to be drawn to the game if you have the first two plus one or more of the following characteristics:

- You believe the soft approach works better with people than the hard one. "Soft" means doing things that satisfy people's needs for respect, recognition, belonging, and self-esteem (Maslow's "higher level" needs). "Hard" means letting people know that if they want to get ahead, or even to keep their jobs, they had better do what they are told. (By doing this you, in effect, threaten their "lower level" needs to make a living and feel secure.)

- You understand that a powerful way to satisfy many of people's higher level needs is to give them a sense of participation in the process that leads to the decisions that affect them.

- You are smart.

- You pick up interaction skills quickly and can use them with some dexterity.

- You are confident. This includes confidence in your ability to fool people about things.

- You think that your ideas about what to do — and how to do it — are usually better than those of the people you work with.

- You get attached to your own ideas and have trouble letting go of them.

The more of these characteristics you have (in addition to the first two), the more susceptible you are to the temptation to play the game.

What can I do to help you resist it?

What makes the temptation hard to resist is that it looks like it doesn't cost you much to play the game, other than a little time. In fact playing it will do a lot of damage to your relationships with people, but they won't make it easy for you to see that. People, especially at work, are reluctant to let on that they were bothered by something you did to or with their ideas.

What helped me to resist the temptation was seeing the costs of playing the game. But this may be harder for you to do than it was for me. I get paid to act as a process observer. When you are not involved in the action you see things you don't see when you are in the middle of it. And people tell you things you normally wouldn't hear.

So here are two examples of what I've seen in my work, each illustrating one of the two most common variations of the game. In one the ultimate objective is to motivate people to be "on your team" in general. In the other it is to create commitment to a specific idea or decision.

Both stories are about smart managers who think they are pretty good with their people (and in fact are in most respects). I hope the stories will give you one or more images that will stay with you and help ward off the temptation to play either version of the game.

HAL AND HIS NOTEBOOKS

The Situation

Hal was a manager who played the game because he thought it would make people feel good to be working for him.

He was a regional sales manager with about twenty people working for him. I met him at a two-day meeting I ran for his boss, the division manager.

About a month after the meeting I got a call from Hal.

He thought I might be able to help him with a problem.

He said that three of his salespeople had told him they were quitting, all in the space of a week.

"They're all top performers," he said, "I hate to lose them, especially right now."

The timing was unfortunate, he said, because he had just launched a new sales strategy to counter moves made by competitors. Losing the three would be a major setback for the effort. He asked if I would be willing to talk to them.

"They may talk to you more freely than they did to me about why they want to leave," he said. "If I understood that better maybe I could talk them into staying. Or at least keep this from becoming a bigger exodus."

He said all he got out of them was that it wasn't the work or the money. Each of them said it was personal reasons, but got vague when he tried to find out more about what these were.

I took the assignment.

I went to the region. I got more information about the situation from Hal. I also got a feeling for how he was with people.

Hal worked long hours. He acted like a person who was very busy, but he made time for anyone who wanted to talk to him. He encouraged his people to tell him how they thought things could be done better, including when these ideas were in disagreement with his decisions.

Hal seemed to do a good job of understanding people's ideas. He recorded them in nicely bound notebooks with leather-look covers.

"May not be able to take advantage of an idea right away," he'd explain as he noted your thought, "but you never know when it will come in handy. Can't remember all the ones I get if I don't write 'em down, this way I don't lose any."

He didn't lose any but he also didn't use any, as I soon found out.

THE INTERVIEWS

I met, individually, with the three people who wanted to leave.

The first one I talked to was Kent. It soon became clear that his personal reasons weren't related to his family situation or to anything else outside the job. When it isn't these things and it's not the work or the money it's usually the boss. I asked how he got along with Hal.

"I get along with him fine," he said, "I just don't like banging my head against a wall. You can't get him to listen when what you say doesn't fall in with his ideas."

I said that in my discussions with Hal he seemed to do a good job of hearing my ideas.

"Yeah, he does that alright," Kent said. "He hears what you say, but he doesn't pay any attention to it. And I sure tried to get him to do that with this new strategy of his."

He said he thought the basic idea behind the strategy was O.K., but he saw serious problems with the way Hal wanted to implement it. And it wasn't just he who thought this, other sales-people agreed with him about it. They also agreed with him about what would be a better way to go about it. But Hal wasn't willing to budge from his tack.

I asked if there had been other occasions on which Hal was unwilling to modify his position. "We all get overly attached to an idea once in a while," I said.

"This is no exception," Kent said, "that's how it is with him. Takes a while to see past his act of welcoming ideas. After people get wise to him they stop telling him what they think. Looks like a few have just stopped thinking. I can't do that, and I have to go fight for my ideas. But you can do that for only so long if it doesn't get you anywhere. The frustration gets to be too much."

After my talk with Kent it occurred to me that Hal assumed making the time to hear what people had to say — and doing a good job of understanding and noting it — was all he needed to do to make them feel he'd done right by their ideas. And that he was then free to put them on a shelf and let them sit there.

I talked to the other two who wanted to quit. That Hal didn't

180

use their ideas was also the main thing pushing them to leave. Both used more de-personalized language than Kent did to talk about what bothered them, but it was clear Hal was the source of their dissatisfaction. One said she felt "shut out of the decision-making process around here." The other said he had come to the conclusion that "this wasn't a place in which people wanted you to have ideas, the thinking was done for you."

■ ■ ■ ■ ■

It was a surprise to Hal that he wasn't getting any return from all the work he put into listening to people's ideas and keeping an accurate record of them. And that these things not only failed to make people feel good, they served to alienate them by creating expectations that were then not met.

To his credit Hal made it easy for me to give him the bad news. He didn't get defensive. He got thoughtful. Perhaps, he said, his problem was that he thought about things too much. He was always thinking about the job, both at work and away from it.

I asked if by this he meant that when he thought about the things that needed to be done he didn't just sketch the broad outlines of plans in his head, he filled in every detail. Leaving no room for other's ideas.

He said yes, that's what he did. And that he could see how putting in all that thought into his ideas also made it hard for him to let go any part of them.

■ ■ ■ ■ ■

Was all this going to make Hal change his ways? I wasn't sure, but there were reasons to be hopeful. This was the first job in which he had to manage people. He'd been at it for only a couple of years so perhaps his ideas about how to do it weren't set in stone. And he understood that what was done with people's ideas had an impact on their motivation, he just hadn't worked out what to do about it.

The next story is about a manager who plays the game to build commitment and support for some specific ideas.

JOAN'S RETREAT

You have an idea you like. You want others to like it too. Instead of trying to sell its charms to them, why not ask them first for their ideas? They might come up with it, and then they'll think it's their idea. If they think that they'll feel more positively about it than if they see it as something imposed on them by you. And if they don't come up with it on their own, you can try to steer their thinking in that direction. If that also doesn't work, you still have the option of imposing it on them. So why not give it a shot?

Because in most cases people will sense that you are playing a game. And then they'll take a lot less kindly to your idea than they would have if you imposed it on them to begin with. This is likely to happen even if you are pretty good at playing the game. As Joan found out.

WHAT JOAN SAID SHE WANTED TO DO

Joan was the president of the Media Services division of a large consulting company. The division designed and managed the production of promotional materials (brochures, point of sales displays) for its customers. When the division was created its goal was to become a leading supplier in a small segment of the overall market for its type of services. Joan felt this goal had been accomplished. It was time to expand into other markets.

She asked me to run a two-day "retreat" for her. She wanted to take the five people who reported to her away from the office to develop an outline of a three-year business plan.

In my pre-session discussions with Joan I asked if she had any ideas about the types of new customers they should go after and, if so, to what extent she wanted the discussion to focus on these versus other ideas.

"What new business we go after is something I'd like

the group to help me decide," she said. "I've got a couple of thoughts, yes, but I'm sure the others do too. I don't think mine should be given any extra weight."

She had a suggestion about how to make sure her ideas didn't unduly influence the others' thinking.

"When it's time to start listing ideas," she said, "call on me last. If I don't have anything to say it'll be because someone else already said it."

A bell should have gone off in my head when she said this, but it didn't. At the time I thought she was just letting me know that as long as her ideas got on the table she didn't care who got the credit for them.

WHAT HAPPENED AT THE SESSION

We get to talking about new business ideas around mid-morning of the first day. I suggest we list them all before we talk about any one in detail. I get a dozen from the group. Joan doesn't add any. It's time to select which ones to grow first. Joan asks me to poll the group. She waits until I note everyone else's votes before she gives me hers.

We get nowhere with the group's top choice. Joan does a great job of helping identify what's going for the idea. She thinks of a couple of non-obvious plusses that haven't occurred to anyone else. None of the others has any serious concerns about making this market a part of their expansion plan, but Joan has a couple.

I write these on a flip-chart and ask people to think of ways to deal with them. They think of several.

"Have they done it?" I ask Joan.

"Yes," she says, "but I see another problem with going after this market."

She tells us what it is. Robert sees a way to fix it. After talking about it for a while Joan agrees that his suggestion might solve that problem. There is, however, one other thing that bothers her about this market segment.

When asked to elaborate she rambles a bit. She talks about things like "the need for cross-segment integrity" and the potential lack of a sustainable customer deficit."

None of us knows what she is talking about. Cynthia takes a guess.

"That's not quite what I meant," Joan says, and rambles a bit more. "Don't know why I'm having trouble explaining it," she says.

I feel we're getting bogged down.

"Would you like some time to find the words for it," I ask Joan. "If so, we can set this idea aside for a while and come back to it later."

"Good suggestion," says Joan.

So we go to work on the idea ranked second.

At first things go as they did with the first idea. Joan leads the way when we talk about why it may be a good customer group to go after. Again she has several concerns about it. But this time she's the first to suggest a way around them.

"It's a bit of a transformation of the idea," she says. "We could get rid of my concerns and preserve a lot of the plusses we've listed if we think about a different but related set of customers."

She describes these customers.

Robert says "I don't see how that segment is related to the one we were talking about. It's a completely different idea, it should be added to the list we made earlier, it doesn't belong in this discussion."

Garren says "I agree with Robert, it's a different idea and we should treat it as such."

Cynthia says "Isn't that the segment you mentioned to me last month?"

Joan doesn't say anything.

So, I think, no one came up with her ideas and now she's trying to lead the group to them. And sees that this isn't working too well. If so, I need to give her a face-saving way to quit playing that game.

"Did I ever get your ideas up on that list?" I ask her. "I know you wanted to be the last in line."

"No, they never did get up," Joan says.

"In that case," I say to her and the others, "we need to change tack."

184

I tell the group what Joan said to me before the session — that she didn't want her ideas to be given any more weight than anyone else's. And that she didn't want to put them out early because when you have an idea in front of you it can keep you from thinking of ones that are different.

"The downside of that," I say to the group, "is that if you *don't* get your ideas out there, it's very hard to be fully open to others."

Robert gives me a look. I think he knows what Joan was doing, and that I'm trying to give her a graceful way to quit doing it.

I turn to Joan.

"To figure out how to proceed," I say, "I need to find out where you stand with your ideas."

It's about ten minutes before we're supposed to break for lunch. Robert looks at his watch and says:

"While you two figure out what to do next, O.K. if the rest of us start our lunch break right now?"

He gets up and starts to leave. Joan says sure. They all leave.

GETTING THE GROUP "BACK IN THE ROOM"

"How do you think they're feeling about the morning?" Joan asks. "Not good," I say.

I tell Joan that for the meeting to be productive we all need to be clear about what room there is for her team's ideas. It's O.K. if she has already decided which new market segments are going to be in the plan, and all she needs is ideas for how best to pursue them.

"For sure I need those kinds of ideas," Joan says, "but I also want the other kind. I've been thinking about two markets, and I think one of them should be in our plan — it's a natural for us, I was sure they'd think of it."

"What about the other idea you have?" I ask.

"Don't have any strong feelings about that one," she says. "And we can get the resources to go after as many as three new segments."

I ask if the one she wants in the plan is the one she mentioned in her transformation of the group's second choice. She says well, yes.

I suggest we add her two ideas to the list and, after lunch, work on the one she likes. Treating it as a separate item, not an extension of anything else.

"Until you settle what to do with that one," I say, "you won't be able to fully appreciate the potential of any other ideas."

I tell the group over lunch what we plan to do after it.

We go to work on Joan's idea after lunch. The others find only a few things to like about it, but have a lot of concerns. I'd told Joan to expect this. I'd also said that it was important that she not let their criticism make her feel defensive. The best way to get them into a more constructive mood than they were in before lunch was to accept the validity of their concerns with her idea and take however much time it took to find good ways of dealing with them — the whole afternoon if need be.

It doesn't take that long to do it, in part because Joan is willing to modify her idea to address some of their concerns.

We spend the rest of the afternoon revisiting the ideas we worked on that morning. It soon becomes clear that Joan's real concern about them has to do with resources: will they have enough to go after both those markets as well as the one she wants in the plan?

They decide the next day that they have the resources to pursue Joan's idea as well as the one that was the group's top choice, plus the idea they voted number four.

■ ■ ■ ■ ■

Joan managed to get out of the two days a plan she liked, and one about which her team seemed to feel positive. Would they have felt more strongly committed to it if Joan had not tried to make them think her idea was the same as one of theirs? And how would they have felt if Joan had not changed her tack, with or without my help? Here's what one person had to say about these things.

Robert and I were the last to leave after the session was over.

"Boy," he said, "did you ever pull her chestnuts out of the flames, at least as far as I'm concerned."

He said he was furious when he realized, before lunch the

186

first day, what she was trying to do. She'd tried something like that on him before. He didn't like it then and he didn't like it this time.

How motivated was he to help Joan make the plan a success?

"I'd help no matter what she did," he said, "that's part of my job. But will I go 'above and beyond'? Not if she keeps playing these games."

■ ■ ■ ■ ■

Variation On the Second Variation

There is one other reason why managers ask for ideas and hope someone will come up with one they have in mind. And this is to reassure themselves that the idea is O.K. The notion here is that if another person, unprompted, comes up with the same idea then it must be a good one.

They think this because they've never stopped to think about the logic behind the notion. If you do, you quickly see that it is flawed because the one thing doesn't have to follow from the other. It may make you feel good to see others arriving at the same conclusion as you, but if you got to it by sloppy thinking they can get to it the same way. So whether they do or don't think of your idea doesn't prove anything about how sound it is.

Logic isn't the only reason to not play this variation of the game. I've talked to people the game has been played with. It isn't hard for them to figure out why they were asked for ideas. And how did they feel when they figured it out?

Irritated and annoyed, they say, certainly not motivated to give the asker any more ideas. But you have to dig to find out these things because people don't like to let you see that they were bothered by something you did with their ideas.

If you want to use others to check the validity of one of your ideas, a more logical and straightforward way is to simply tell them what it is and ask if they see anything wrong with it. And if so, how to fix it.

187

INVITING IDEAS ONLY WHEN YOU'RE OPEN TO THEM

Two Other Things to Keep in Mind

- *You won't win the game even if they **do** come up with your ideas*

It's very hard to make people think they played a bigger role than they actually did in helping you decide something. This is the case even when it appears that you've succeeded — you asked for ideas hoping people would give you the one you have in mind, and they did just that.

But almost always something in your tone of voice or body language will give away the game, either right then or when they hear you talk about the idea again later. It's especially hard to not give away the game if you're the boss.

People tend to be very tuned in to the signals the boss gives, wittingly or unwittingly. They'll figure out that they didn't really give you the idea, it's one you had all along. What's worse, they may decide to go along with the fiction. The boss wants us to think we got our way on this one? Okay, we'll pretend that's how it is. And then of course the only person who is fooled about what's happening is the boss.

- *You don't have to be open to ideas all the time*

There will be times when you feel you don't want any more ideas from anyone, you've got some that are good enough for what needs to be done. It's time to stop inventing and start implementing.

There will also be times — as was the case with Joan — when you are temporarily not open to others' ideas because you have one you like, and you need to put it to rest before you can entertain anything different.

Whatever the reason, when you are *not* open to ideas it's best to tell people this. Doing this won't diminish their motivation to help you, if it isn't something you do all the time. If, more often than not, you do invite and make use of people's ideas, they won't be upset to find that sometimes you're closed to them. In fact it will have the opposite effect. They will appreciate your candor, and it will reassure them that when you do ask for ideas you're not playing a game.

INVITE IDEAS ONLY WHEN YOU'RE OPEN TO THEM: VERY QUICK REVIEW SUMMARY

It can be tempting to invite ideas when you're *not* open to them, because it looks like an easy way to build commitment to a decision or relationship.

But if you don't really want the ideas then you're just playing a game. It's a game at which you have a lot to lose and very little to gain. I hope the stories in the chapter have convinced you of this, enough to help you resist the temptation.

■ Appendix 1:
Additional Practice Notes

Practice — how, and how much?

The more you use a rule the more it will become a part of your habits of thought and interaction, something you do without having to think much about when or how to do it.

You may find that this happens relatively quickly and easily with some of the rules. Reading about them once may be all it takes for you to start using them. The first few times you use any one of them you may have to think about what you are doing, but it's not long before using it becomes just the way you are with people.

With other rules you may find that it's harder to start using them and that, after you do start, it takes longer to make using them a habit.

Which rules will you take to easily, and which less easily? The answer is different for different people. It depends, in part, on which rules feel most like a natural extension of the way you do things anyway, and which feel the most different. It also depends on the timing.

At any given stage of our personal development we are more ready to add some things to our "bag of tools" than others. The things you want to add to that bag can be likened to fruit on a tree — you can make the ripest ones fall into the bag with the least effort.

Given all of the above, how should you go about making the rules a part of the way you do things?

One answer is to do what comes naturally. Go with whatever

you take to easily after reading the book. Pick up the book again from time to time, and re-read the parts you feel prompted to read — or just the part where the book happens to fall open.

A very different answer to the question is, of course, that you should go about the practice in a more deliberate and organized way. For example, if you agree that the first two rules are at the core of what you need to do to tap minds and hearts, then shouldn't you focus first on adding those two to your bag, regardless of whether you take to them easily? And should you have a practice plan to follow, similar to an exercise or diet regimen?

Create the mix that's right for you

There is something to be said for the do-what-comes-naturally approach. It makes you focus on what feels right for your particular style, situation, and stage of development. The difficulty with this approach is that it can be hard to tell when you're being guided by these considerations, and when you're taking the path of least resistance. Doing the easy thing can also feel like the "right" thing to be doing, even when it isn't what you need to do in your circumstances.

What the "practice plan" approach has going for it is that it makes you focus on adding things to your bag in the order in which they will give you the biggest return for the time and effort you put into it. The thing to look out for with this approach is the tendency to let the plan take over. Sticking with the plan can become the object of the exercise, even when the plan you picked turns out to be one that doesn't suit you.

The most effective approach to practice is usually a blend of these two. How do you find the blend that's right for you?

If you usually take the do-what-comes-naturally approach, do the practice in a bit more organized and deliberate way. If you normally like to develop and follow plans with defined objectives and mileposts, back off a little and pay more attention to what feels right to you, right now. The right mix is usually one that doesn't feel either too easy or too hard. You can think of it as the path of "right resistance."

Give yourself a mistake quota

The rules that feel the most different from the way you usually do something may be the ones you stand to gain the most from if you adopt them. What can make you hesitate to try them out is the worry that when you do you'll look awkward, or that you'll make the situation worse if you aren't able to make them work. What if you invite criticism of one of your ideas and, when you get it, forget how best to handle it?

There are two things you can do to address these concerns:

- Keep in mind that there are two parts to using the rules — the "how to," and the accompanying mindset or frame of mind. If you maintain the right mindset, then the odds are that you will make a positive impact on the situation and the people in it even if you make a hash of the "how to." Not as big a positive impact as when you get both things right, but not one that's negative.

- Pick practice settings in which you feel it isn't critical to "get it right the first time." There is truth to the saying that we learn by "trial and error." Kids learn things fast because they feel free to fool around with what they're trying to learn, without worrying about how many errors they make. There aren't many situations in which we, as adults, feel free to make errors, but that doesn't mean we can't find or create some in which we *can* feel free to do so. You could, for example:

  - *Find a practice "partner" — someone at work or outside it with whom you feel comfortable trying things you may not have got quite right. Whether or not you tell this "partner" what you're doing depends on the kind of relationship you have with that person, and on whether you think he or she has anything to gain from knowing it.*

  - *Put together a practice group — you plus two or more other people who would also like to practice using some of these rules (or something else). The "group" could, of course, be just you and one other person — a practice partner who also wants to practice something.*

193

- *Try things out in workshops you attend, especially those in which you are asked to discuss things in small groups or teams.*

- *Try things out in activities such as "brainstorming" meetings in which you can be less careful than usual about what you say or do.*

Keep it simple

The process of incorporating the rules into your way of doing things will go quicker and more easily if you focus your attention on just a few things at a time.

Keep in mind what was said earlier about limiting to three the number of things you have to remember to do on any one occasion. It's a useful rule of thumb not just when you want to make something a part of your golf or tennis swing, but also when you want to make something a part of your interaction habits.

Have some fun with it

When you practice using the rules you'll find, more often than not, that the activity is self-reinforcing. You'll get a good idea out of it, or see that you made a positive impact on someone, or feel good about having kept your balance when someone trashed one of your ideas. This will give you an incentive to continue the practice.

You can add to the incentive by building some fun into it. For example, if you want to focus on managing the ego agenda, look for meetings in which you don't have to be "on" all the time. Step back from the action now and then and see if you can spot people playing ego agenda driven games. Or toss a few pebbles and watch for ripples. In the early part of a meeting, take some pains to point out what you think are the plusses of someone's ideas. See what attitude that person takes toward your ideas later on. Notice whether a relative stranger responds in kind more easily than someone you work with often and who is used to trashing your ideas.

It can also be fun to exercise your imagination. The next time you feel you could do with a fresh idea, take a five minute idea-growing break. Think of a totally impractical idea, ideally one that makes you laugh. ("Get closer to customers by legally adopting their kids.") Practice transforming the idea. (It will help if you write down the plusses of the idea on a piece of paper ... or put them on your screen.) Keep in mind that the main object of the exercise is to stretch some mental muscles, and not to produce an idea you can use. If you get one out of the exercise, great. If not, you've seeded your imagination with some thoughts that may bear fruit later.

Use them flexibly

You'll make your practice both more interesting and more profitable if you include in it some variations on the themes. Say, for example, that you want to grow someone's idea. But you have the feeling that the other person expects you to have a concern that you do indeed have about the idea, and that until you voice that concern nothing else you say is going to be fully heard. So in this case, *don't* talk first about what you think is going for the idea, do this *after* you acknowledge the concern.

In general, feel free to modify the way you use any of the rules in any given situation.

Keep the ultimate goal in mind

Using the rules described in this book will make you a more effective manager of innovation at the operational level. It will help you to get resources and motivate people to do the work needed to make specific innovations happen. It won't guarantee that you'll be successful in doing these things in every situation or with every person in it, but it will significantly increase your batting average.

■ Appendix 2: Memory Joggers

This appendix includes:

- A diagrammatic reminder of what the rules are about (see next page).

- A review of key themes.

- A what-to-do-when map.

- A collection of the At-A-Glance summaries.

DIAGRAMMATIC REMINDER OF WHAT THE RULES DO FOR YOU

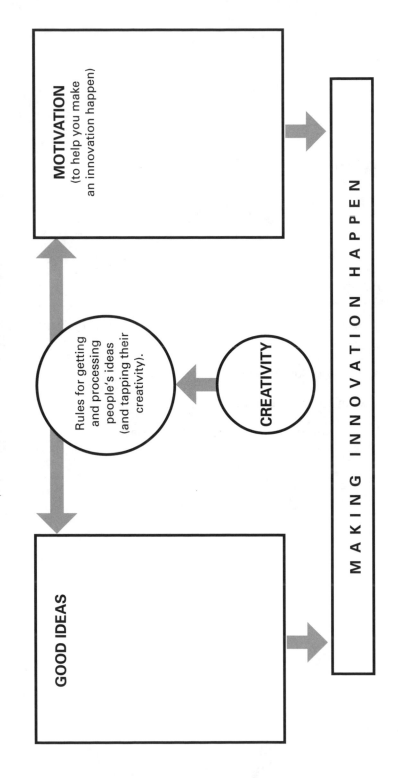

MAKING INNOVATION HAPPEN – REVIEW OF KEY THEMES

It's not enough to have a good idea

Innovation is the introduction of something new or different. It starts with an idea — someone sees a better way to satisfy your customers' needs, or to improve something in your organization. But to put a new product or process in place you need more than these ideas plus a good plan of action. You also have to get people to embrace the ideas — both the people who must approve them before you can proceed, and those whose help you need to implement them. This is not an easy task.

It's not an easy task because the same economic forces that push your organization to innovate also push it to run lean. The people who have to approve your innovation project tend to be stingy with the resources they make available to you. Both you and the people on your implementation "team" usually have to find time for the project while still taking care of your regular jobs.

Even if you're all assigned full-time to the project, you rarely have all the resources and time you'd like for it. The pace at which you have to work, and the time you have to put in are like those needed to start a new business on a limited budget. What's different is that you can't give people shares of stock in the venture. So you have to find other ways to motivate them to put in the level of effort it takes to make the venture successful.

What you do with people's ideas has a big impact on your effectiveness

Even in the leanest organizations, there are people who have a knack for making innovation happen. If you observe these "naturals" for a while you see that a big factor in their success is that they know how to draw on others' ideas and knowledge in a way that does two things. It nets them useful ideas and insights. And it enables them to

199

tap some powerful sources of motivation, as follows:

- The way they listen and respond to others' ideas says to them: I value and respect your thinking, and therefore *you*.

- Their ability to tap people's creative side makes working with them an affirming experience for those people.

- They create a climate in which people feel it's both safe and productive to express "half-baked" thoughts that they would normally keep to themselves. This makes working with them both less stressful and more energizing than working with someone with whom you have to watch what you say, because it might be held against you.

What these "naturals" understand, in essence, is that you can get to people's hearts through their minds.

You can't fake it

The rules described in this book enable you to do what the "naturals" do. But to make them work your interest in people's ideas and opinions has to be real. This means:

- You're open to idea help. You're open because you're in charge of your ego agenda — you know that asking others for ideas doesn't mean you don't have good ones of your own, and this makes you secure enough to not worry that people might think otherwise.
  You're also open because you know that when you ask for ideas, you're not inviting people to tell you what to do — you know how to keep them off your decision turf.

- You know that others — including those with less knowledge, experience, or smarts than you — can help add depth or breadth or freshness to your thinking.

- You resist the temptation to make people think you're open to their ideas when you're not. You know that if you don't do it too often, it's O.K. to *not* be open to others' ideas on occasion — letting them know it when this is the case reassures them that when you *do* ask for ideas you're not playing games.

It's hard to make people think you want their ideas when you don't or that ideas really theirs. The attempt to fool them in these ways almost always backfires, you decrease, not increase their motivation to help you get things done. People don't always let you know they weren't fooled, especially if you're the boss. In such cases the only person who is fooled about what happened is apt to be the boss.

■ ■ ■ ■ ■

USING THE RULES – A WHAT-TO-DO-WHEN MAP

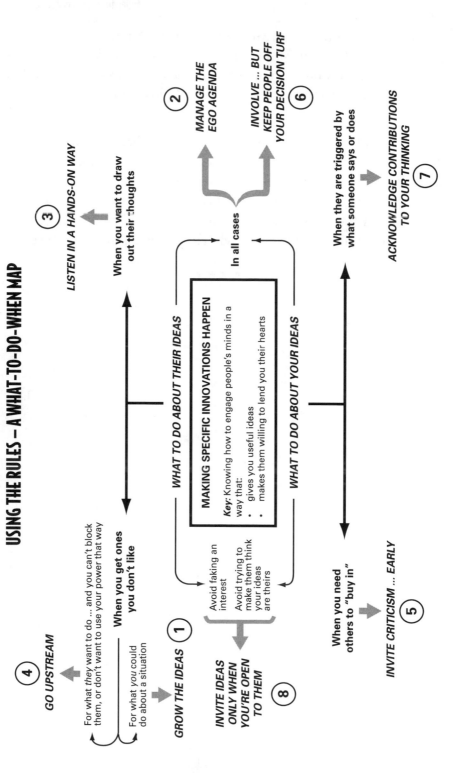

GROW THE IDEAS ①

GO UPSTREAM ④

When you get ones you don't like

For what *they* want to do ... and you can't block them, or don't want to use your power that way

For what *you* could do about a situation

INVITE IDEAS ONLY WHEN YOU'RE OPEN TO THEM ⑧

Avoid faking an interest

Avoid trying to make them think your ideas are theirs

MAKING SPECIFIC INNOVATIONS HAPPEN

Key: Knowing how to engage people's minds in a way that:
- gives you useful ideas
- makes them willing to lend you their hearts

WHAT TO DO ABOUT THEIR IDEAS

WHAT TO DO ABOUT YOUR IDEAS

In all cases

When you want to draw out their thoughts

LISTEN IN A HANDS-ON WAY ③

MANAGE THE EGO AGENDA ②

INVOLVE ... BUT KEEP PEOPLE OFF YOUR DECISION TURF ⑥

When they are triggered by what someone says or does

ACKNOWLEDGE CONTRIBUTIONS TO YOUR THINKING ⑦

When you need others to "buy in"

INVITE CRITICISM ... EARLY ⑤

COLLECTION OF AT-A-GLANCE SUMMARIES

The At-A-Glance summaries are reproduced on the following pages. Also listed, along with each summary, is the page on which you can find the full Quick Review Summary for that rule.

There are no At-A-Glance summaries for Rules 6 and 8, because the Quick Review summaries fit on one page. You'll find these in this collection, for these two rules, in lieu of any At-A-Glance summaries.

1

THE IDEA GROWING PROCESS: AT-A-GLANCE SUMMARY

Part A: Appraisal that adds value

1. **Find the "seeds" (what's going for the idea?)**
    a) Put the idea in quotes ("...")
    b) Identify "3–5" potential advantages (dig for 1–2 that are non-obvious.)

    Key: give yourself time to think.

2. **Decide how you want to grow the idea**
    a) Identify the flaw(s) (up to 3, if necessary)
    b) Select the fork you want to take (tailor or transform?)
    c) Pose the right question.

    Example of c): if you want to tailor and the big flaw is high cost, is the question how to justify it? How to reduce cost? Other?

Part B: Tailoring or Transforming

Just one step here — tailor or transform as per the question(s) you pose in Part A.

To tailor: modify (by adding or subtracting bits, or by changing the manner or circumstances in which you pursue the idea).
To transform: metamorphose (by thinking of a *different* way of going after one or more plusses of the initial idea).

Things to keep in mind:

*   *If after several "tailorings" you still don't have an acceptable idea, back up and take the other fork (transform the idea).*
*   *Be actively engaged in the process, don't sit back and wait for others to fix the flaws for you.*
*   *Let the idea change, don't "set it in stone."*

For complete Quick Review Summary, turn to page 38.

2

MANAGING THE EGO AGENDA:
AT-A-GLANCE SUMMARY OF THE HOW

With others: Change how you act, don't try to change how they react

- Cultivate the "no, but ..." response
  ("It's not acceptable as is, but let me tell you what I think it has going for it ...")

- Resist the temptation to tell them what you see
  (It's hard to get people to see the ego agenda games they play.)

Dealing with your own ego agenda

- Keep your balance
  - keep an eye on the "temperature under your collar"
  - remember you hit your best shots when you are balanced.
- Rethink your looking-good strategies
  - When in doubt, ask yourself if it:
    - is based on looking good by making others look less good?
    - involves taking more than your fair share of things like air-time or credit for ideas?
    - keeps you from getting the most out of others' ideas?
      (You can't afford to keep it if any of the answers is "yes.")
  - The core of an effective strategy:

    Compete against yourself, not others.

For complete Quick Review Summary, turn to page 78.

3

DOING MORE HANDS-ON LISTENING:
AT-A-GLANCE SUMMARY

When to switch from the auto to the manual mode	How to clarify or dig for the other's thought

When you're looking for ideas AND:

You find yourself thinking or saying "It's the same as my idea — nothing new there" Listen for the difference
- either talk about your idea, then ask others in what ways theirs' may be different
- or first ask others to say more about their idea, you listen for and talk about the differences

You are asked for information about the situation for which you want ideas Dig for the thought beneath the question:
- answer the question briefly, then draw out the other person "What were you thinking?"

For complete Quick Review Summary, turn to page 100.

4

GOING UPSTREAM (vs GROWING IDEAS): AT-A-GLANCE SUMMARY

Situation		Response
When faced with an idea you don't like, and it is:		
A suggestion about what *you* could do about a situation.		**Grow it:** Say what you think is going for it, talk about your concern(s) ... then tailor or transform.
Something the other person wants to do AND you either don't have the power to block it, or don't want to use it.		**Go upstream:** Understand the ends the other person is trying to attain by doing that think ... then suggest another way to attain them, a way that's also O.K. with you. "May I ask why ...?"

For complete Quick Review Summary, turn to page 117.

5

EXPOSING YOUR IDEAS TO CRITICISM:
AT-A-GLANCE SUMMARY OF THE HOW

Dealing with the concerns

Type of concern	Way to respond
Is based on a misunderstanding	Clarify idea or situation it's designed to address
Requires problem-solving	Find a way to address the concern that's acceptable to you and to the other person
Needs acknowledgement but not problem-solving	Make sure you understand it, show empathy, and if you can, make it easier for the other to live with it

Maintaining a non-defensive stance

Remember it's your show

Make a mental cue-card
An image related to a metaphor that:

- Feels apt
- Is appealing
- Reminds you it's your show

Know when to show yourself the card
You are being defensive if you try to counter others' concerns ... the two most common ways of doing this are:

- Minimizing them
- Trying to offset them by selling your idea's strong points

For complete Quick Review Summary, turn to page 147.

6

INVOLVE PEOPLE, BUT KEEP THEM OFF YOUR DECISION TURF: QUICK REVIEW SUMMARY

There are two ways to create ownership in and commitment to a plan of action:

- give people votes or vetoes in the decisions that need to be made in the plan development process;
- help them to contribute useful ideas to the plan.

Use of the rules in the preceding chapters enables you to take the second path, which is better because it:

- helps you preserve your right to decide what goes in your action plan;
- leads to commitment to help you that goes beyond what you get from a sense of ownership alone.

Keeping bosses off your decision turf

- Involve them ... sufficiently ... in the right activity.
- Tailor the approach to the boss.
- If they insist, take them "upstream."

If you give people votes, don't get locked into the "majority rule"

- If it's about which ideas to grow, don't go strictly by the numbers. (Twelve luke-warm votes may count for less than three passionate ones.)
- Let people know the rules of your voting game.

Be clear about which turf you want to protect

- Be guided not just by whether you're a boss or a subordinate, but also by the other specifics of the situation.
- To avoid unnecessary turf fights, keep in mind who thinks which decision belongs to them (in the plan development process).

(No additional At-A-Glance Summary.)

7

ACKNOWLEDGING CONTRIBUTIONS:
AT-A-GLANCE SUMMARY OF THE HOW

• If it isn't clear to others that something they gave you *is a useful addition to your thinking,* let them know that.

And if it isn't clear that what you got *was derived from something they said or did,* let them know this also.

• How you acknowledge the contribution is simple. You can say something like:

"You just gave me an idea ..."

or,

"I hadn't thought of that, I'll look into it. Thanks."

or,

"Thanks for that piece of information you sent me, it helped clarify the problem."

• Both the contribution and the acknowledgment can be made in face-to-face discussions, or in other ways.

• In general, let people know you got something useful from them right after you get it, or as soon after that as is possible and appropriate.

For complete Quick Review Summary, turn to page 171.

8

INVITE IDEAS ONLY WHEN YOU'RE OPEN TO THEM: VERY QUICK REVIEW SUMMARY

It can be tempting to invite ideas when you're *not* open to them, because it looks like an easy way to build commitment to a decision or relationship.

But if you don't really want the ideas then you're just playing a game. It's a game at which you have a lot to lose and very little to gain. I hope the stories in the chapter have convinced you of this, enough to help you resist the temptation.

(No additional At-A-Glance Summary.)

Notes

Notes

Notes